SECOND
RELEASE

WHEN A
BAND-AID
Is No
LONGER
ENOUGH

YOU'RE RIGHT
I'M WRONG

JEFFRY MARINELLI

WHY BUY THE BOOK

This book is about setting Realistic Expectations

This book is not just a collection of insights; it's a blueprint for taking actionable steps to repair, rebuild, and strengthen your partnership. Through real-world scenarios, practical tools, and proven strategies. It offers a practical roadmap to break free from destructive patterns and create a thriving, fulfilling relationship. This book empowers you to navigate and mend the complexities of your relationship, fostering understanding, communication, and positive change.

Discover a revolutionary perspective on your partner you never knew existed. With a fresh approach to shaping future decisions for improved outcomes. This book provides profound insights into your partner's expectations, unraveling the reasons and methods through which you may fall short.

Uncover the profound insights within this book as you delve into your partner's four fundamental essential needs for happiness. Gain a deep understanding of the pitfalls that contribute to relationship deterioration and explore the stages your partner may undergo to sustain the connection.

Wondering why your partner seems elusive, reacting strongly to minor issues, and feeling like you're failing to make them happy? Ever faced the dilemma of your partner retreating to the bedroom in frustration, leaving you to ponder whether to give them space or knock and apologize?

Quick test: Your partner is upset and locks the door. What's your move?
A. Leave them be to cool off or
B. Knock on the door and apologize.
If you picked A, brace yourself for a revelation in this book.

The correct answer is later in the book. This book is your guide to a fulfilling and happy life.

This book was carefully writen for all genders and partnerships, including if you're single, seeking to improve a current relationship, or start a new one, this book offers insights. Break free from the unnecessary games hindering connection. It's time to revamp your relationship and take a new approach.

Published by Art and Living, Los Angeles, California
https://youarerightiamwrong.com

Printed in the United States of America
Hardback ISBN 978-2-59552-330-0
Ebook ISBN 978-2-99619-848-0
Paperback ISBN 978-3-00-689107-0

The publisher and the author provide this book and its contents on an "as is" basis and make no representations or warranties of any kind concerning this book or its contents. The publisher and the author disclaim all such representations and warranties, including but not limited to warranties of healthcare for a particular purpose. In addition, the publisher and the author assume no responsibility for errors, inaccuracies, omissions, or any other inconsistencies herein.

The content of this book is for informational purposes only and is not intended to diagnose, treat, cure, or prevent any condition or disease. You understand that this book is not intended as a substitute for consultation with a licensed practitioner. Please consult with your physician or healthcare specialist regarding the suggestions and recommendations made in this book. The use of this book implies your acceptance of this disclaimer.

The publisher and the author make no guarantees concerning the level of success you may experience by following the advice and strategies contained in this book. You accept the risk that results will differ for each individual. The testimonials and examples provided in this book show exceptional results, which may not apply to the average reader. They are not intended to represent or guarantee that you will achieve the same or similar results.

You're Right, I'm Wrong

There's always HOPE

You're Right, I'm Wrong

PART 1: Unraveling Relationship Challenges:

The author delves into the critical aspects that contribute to relationship challenges. Let's start with "Navigating the Path to Shared Happines," setting the tone for an honest exploration of relationship dynamics. Then, we tackle the four common mistakes couples often make: neglecting or ignoring a partner, adopting an entitled attitude, setting false expectations, and engaging in lies and secrets. But here's the key for mistake, there's a corresponding solution. Moving on, we hit the four stages of relationship decline: Adjusting, Selfishness, Disrespect, and Incompatibility. Forget the jargon – this is about understanding why things go south and getting a roadmap for a positive transformation.

PART 2: Foundations of Successful Relationships

We shift the focus to essential skills and understanding crucial for a happy relationship. Explore key skills like asking the question, making good choices, compromising, and effective communication in Four Skills for a Happy Relationship. Each skill is elaborated upon to empower you with practical tools for relationship success. Dive into individual happiness needs—preferences, dislikes, areas of improvement, and things you hate in Your Needs to Be Happy. Then, delve into your partner's happiness needs, emphasizing the pillars of balance, equality, security, and trust. This section is your go-to manual for crafting a robust foundation, ensuring a satisfying partnership built on mutual understanding and effective communication.

PART 3: Reset: Empowering Your Partnership

We focus on practical tools for daily use to restore balance, equality, security, and trust in your relationship. Explore tools for relationship balance, covering managing friendships, habits, hobbies, sports, and work to keep your partnership well-rounded. Discover tools for relationship equality, from reducing arguments to bridging beliefs, showing appreciation, and sharing responsibilities. Find daily tools ensuring relationship security, including feeling loved, managing stress, controlling temper, and addressing weight concerns. Finally, equip yourself with daily tools for relationship trust, covering boundaries, lifestyle choices, avoiding second-guessing, and being cautious of white lies. This section provides a practical roadmap for implementing positive changes in your daily life and strengthening your partnership.

Contents

CHAPTER 9: SECURITY PILLAR
Daily Tools for Relationship Security

Baggage Issues & Tools to repair The Security Pillar

CHAPTER 10: TRUST PILLAR
Daily Tools for Relationship Trust

Baggage Issues & Tools to repair The Trust Pillar

About the Author
Jeff Marinelli ...

Jeff Marinelli, an author and magazine publisher, is on a mission to positively impact his marriage, family, and philanthropic endeavors. Central to his philosophy is the unwavering commitment to alleviate stress for his partner, epitomizing the sentiment, "MY WIFE IS MY LIFE."

While leading a dynamic team of high-tech, high-touch professionals in his business endeavors, Jeff finds immense joy in fostering thriving relationships. Not a psychologist by trade, he identifies as an optimist who draws insights from profound personal and professional experiences shared with his wife.

His wife, a super-achiever with a track record of collaborating with some of the world's most influential entrepreneurs, has excelled in growing and selling multimillion-dollar businesses. Despite her demanding, aggressive, and intimidating demeanor to others, Jeff's focus on love and openness, anchored in the fundamental principle of trust, has allowed their friendship, love, and marriage to flourish. Together, they form an inseparable and committed duo dedicated to maintaining alignment in their decision-making processes.

About the Artist
Gonzalo Duran...

Gonzalo Duran, a renowned Angeleno artist with a global following, traces his roots back to Mexico but found his artistic home in the United States. Emigrating as a child, he grew up in East L.A., later honing his skills at Otis Art Institute and Chouinard Art School. Often hailed as the Marc Chagall of North and Central Americas, Gonzalo captivates audiences with his brilliant and occasionally startling palette, a perfect complement to his boundless imagination.

At the heart of his artistic endeavors is the Mosaic Tile House, a creative haven co-run with his wife, artist Cheri Pann, in their Venice, California, residence. Gonzalo's life is a testament to the principles espoused in this book – recognizing that his partner's happiness translates to his own.

Intricately weaving the visual narrative of the book through his artworks, Gonzalo shares a gift with the reader. His creations showcase his artistic prowess and serve as a visible embodiment of the book's essence. As an artist living the philosophy expressed in these pages, Gonzalo Duran adds a unique and authentic dimension to the profound message.

PART 1:

How Did It Get So Bad

EROSIONS OF LOVE
DO YOU THINK I LOVE YOU?
DO YOU LIKE HOW I TREAT YOUR FAMILY
DO YOU LIKE ME?
DO YOU THINK WE TREAT EACH OTHER WITH RESPECT?
DO YOU LIKE HOW I TREAT YOUR FRIENDS?
DO YOU LIKE MY FAMILY?
COULD WE HAVE A BETTER PARTNERSHIP?
DO YOU SEE US TOGETHER FOREVER?
DO YO LIKE HOW I TREAT YOU?
DO YOU LIKE MY FRIENDS?
DO YOU STILL LOVE ME?
DO YOU THINK I'M FUN?

Chapter 1:
Erosion of Love

Erosion of Love

**Happiness is an inside job,
and it's not your partner's responsibility to make you happy.**

This book will guide you in understanding that happiness goes both ways in a relationship. It emphasizes that your partner isn't solely responsible for your happiness; it is a shared responsibility. The book encourages you to take an active role in ensuring your partner's happiness while also focusing on your own. It aims to help you become a better partner by fostering mutual happiness and strengthening the bond in your relationship.

Have you found yourself needing help with your partner's happiness, their thoughts, or the reasons behind seemingly trivial conflicts? Does the once-idyllic life now feel like an overwhelming, complicated, and thankless task?

Upon entering our partnerships, many of us needed a deeper understanding of what genuinely brings happiness to our partners. The common misconception that providing a good life through hard work should suffice often proves inadequate, leading to a sense of dissatisfaction. However, fundamentally, individuals yearn for shared happiness – the kind that stems from compatibility, companionship, and straightforward enjoyment.

This book guides you to achieving that great life with your partner without unnecessary complications. It's about rediscovering the person your partner fell in love with, reigniting that spark. To do this, you'll explore the foundations of a successful relationship, navigating potential challenges to create a deeply connected, honest, and loving partnership.

This book aims to unravel the intricacies of your partner's thoughts, helping you navigate potential challenges with care and love, particularly during the less-than-ideal moments or unforeseen issues. Whether you feel a disconnect with your partner or sense there's room for improvement in your relationship, this book is tailored for you. It delves into the nuances of daily life with your partner, offering insights into making thoughtful choices, fostering effective communication, and mastering the art of problem-solving.

Even if you think your occasional arguments are standard, this book will reveal how it can help you navigate through them. It's about transforming your partnership into something not just functional but extraordinary.

I may not have a formal degree in psychology, but I've built a strong, lasting partnership through decades of real-life experience. The practical advice I've gathered and shared with friends has proven helpful, and now I'm sharing it with you in this book.

You're Right, I'm Wrong is an easy-to-read guide filled with relatable, everyday examples drawn from real-life situations. It begins with the empowering idea that you have the ability to take the lead in improving your relationship. By approaching the book with an open mind and focusing on the parts that resonate with you, you'll find actionable steps to create meaningful change. This book provides a straightforward path for anyone looking to realign their relationship.

The shared experiences and insights will remind you of important truths you may already know but haven't fully put into practice. It also sheds light on the pain of dealing with an unhappy partner and helps you uncover the underlying causes.

By the end of the book, you'll have an understanding of the dynamics at play and the tools to make a difference to transform your relationship.

TO CHANGE ONE LIFE

Early one morning, an old man was walking along the shore after a big storm had passed and found the vast beach littered with starfish, stretching in both directions as far as the eye could see. Off in the distance, the old man noticed a small boy approaching. As the boy walked along the beach, he paused every so often, bending down to pick up an object to throw it into the sea.

As the boy came closer, the man called out, "Good morning! May I ask what it is that you are doing?" The young boy looked up and replied, "Throwing starfish into the ocean. The tide has washed them up onto the beach, and they can't return to the sea by themselves. When the sun gets high, they will die unless I throw them back into the water." The old man replied, "But there must be tens of thousands of starfishes on this beach. I'm afraid you won't be able to make much of a difference.

"The boy bent down, picked up yet another starfish and threw it as far as he could into the ocean. Then he turned, smiled, and said, "It made a difference to that one!"

Chapter 2:
Four Mistakes – Four Solutions

In the dynamics of a partnership, inevitable mistakes don't always erupt with drama or immediate consequence. More often, they creep in quietly, subtly eroding the trust, intimacy, and balance that hold a relationship together. These aren't always grand betrayals or explosive fights—but repeated small missteps that, if unchecked, can unravel the emotional fabric of a partnership over time.

Let's delve into four common, yet overlooked, mistakes that can slowly fracture even the strongest relationships:

Mistake 1: Neglecting Your Partner
This insidious habit unfolds by overlooking fundamental needs—companionship, communication, intimacy, love, and presence. Imagine dismissing dinner plans with your partner due to exhaustion yet prioritizing a game with a friend.

Neglecting to celebrate achievements, big or small, creates an emotional void. Partners need acknowledgment and recognition for their efforts. Imagine accomplishing a personal or professional milestone without any acknowledgment or celebration from your partner.

Neglecting personal growth and development within the relationship can hinder its progress. Imagine staying stagnant without effort to improve oneself or contribute positively to the partnership's growth.

Overlooking emotional needs, such as providing support during challenging times, can create emotional distance. Imagine your partner going through a difficult situation, and you fail to offer comfort or understanding, leaving them feeling alone in their struggles.

A lack of physical and verbal affection can lead to feelings of neglect. Imagine going days without expressing love, appreciation, or physical touch, leaving your partner feeling unloved and disconnected.

Mistake 2: Entitlement
An attitude of exemption from responsibilities harms the relationship. While entitlement may have advantages elsewhere, it erodes the foundations of partnerships. Imagine neglecting chores while citing your with fun activities.

One partner consistently leaves chores, errands, or parenting duties to the other, justifying it with statements like:I work more hours., I'm too tired., I had a rough day—I deserve a break, You're better at this stuff anyway."

When one person expects constant appreciation but rarely gives it—"You should be grateful I even did this"—while neglecting to recognize their partner's contributions, that creates resentment.

Taking each other for granted and forgetting to express gratitude can diminish the joy in the relationship. Imagine never expressing appreciation for the little things your partner does, leading to a lack of positive reinforcement.

Mistake 3: False Expectations
Consistently establishing and then failing to meet expectations undermines trust. Picture committing to return home within an hour but consistently arriving three hours later. This pattern of behavior not only strains the partnership but can escalate to a level where your partner struggles to rely on your word.

Please prioritize quality time together to avoid emotional drift. Imagine consistently choosing other activities over spending meaningful moments with your partner, leading to isolation."

Mistake 4: Lies and Secrets
In a partnership, honesty is the foundation of emotional safety—the invisible glue that holds intimacy and connection together. When we start bending the truth with small omissions or so-called "white lies," we may tell ourselves it's harmless, even protective. But underneath that reasoning is often fear: fear of conflict, fear of judgment, or fear of disappointing our partner.

But here's the truth: white lies, even when well-intended, create cracks in the relationship. They quietly undermine the very trust we depend on to feel secure, seen, and valued.

You and your partner agree on a tight financial plan to save for something meaningful—a home, a trip, getting out of debt. But then, you give money to a family member without telling your partner because "it's not that much" or "they really needed it." At first, it feels like a private decision. But once discovered, the issue is no longer just about the money—it's about the breach of trust, the withholding of truth, and the unspoken message: "My choice mattered more than our agreement."

Mistake 1:

Neglecting or Ignoring Your Partner

Neglecting or Ignoring Your Partner

Neglect in a relationship manifests when a partner's needs are overlooked. It's crucial that your partner feels not only appreciated but also genuinely wanted. A partner who perceives their life is intertwined with yours is less likely to feel neglected; they feel loved, appreciated, and supported.

Daily life brings various challenges—family matters, friends, health, hobbies, work, etc. Your choices in handling these aspects can either balance or tip the scales, affecting your partner's sense of priority and care. Neglect often arises when your partner feels their concerns are overshadowed by other commitments.

What does neglect look like in different aspects of life?

Family: Taking sides in disagreements, prioritizing family events over your partner's preferences, or spending more time with your family than your partner can lead to neglect.

Friends: Oversharing information about your partner, spending excessive time with friends, or turning to friends instead of your partner in times of need are signs of neglect.

Hobbies and Sports: Dedicating too much time to personal interests at the expense of quality time with your partner, especially if they are interested in different activities, can lead to neglect.

Parenting: Unequal sharing of responsibilities, assuming your partner has everything covered, or being absent during crucial family activities can contribute to neglect.

Communication: Dismissing your partner's need to talk, feeling too busy to listen, or believing their concerns are insignificant are signs of neglect.

Work: Working excessively, prioritizing work over family commitments, or neglecting special occasions for work-related reasons can lead to neglect.

Quality Time: Being physically present but emotionally distant, not engaging with your partner's needs, or providing them with only your leftover energy are indicators of neglect.

Personal Issues: Struggling with addiction, depression, or past trauma can limit the emotional energy available for your partner, leading to neglect. Neglect often goes unnoticed; partners may communicate their feelings through subtle signs. Ignoring these signs can result in a partner feeling unheard, unappreciated, and, eventually, neglected.

If these patterns persist, they can trigger the Four Stages of Relationship Decline, leading to significant changes in your partner's feelings and behavior. Awareness of these stages is crucial for understanding the potential consequences of neglect.

To counteract neglect, demonstrate your presence, care, and appreciation daily. Simple gestures, such as bringing coffee in the morning or preparing a warm welcome after a tough day, can significantly impact you. Be engaged at home, avoid distractions, and listen actively to your partner's concerns.

The solution lies in achieving a balanced partnership where both partners share responsibilities, and support each other emotionally.

Neglect isn't always loud—it's often the quiet absence of effort, attention, and emotional presence. It accumulates in the spaces where connection should exist: the conversations that don't happen, the support that's missing, the moments that go unacknowledged. Over time, these absences speak louder than words.

But just as neglect builds gradually, so too can reconnection. The key lies in conscious, consistent presence. Relationships thrive when both partners feel seen, heard, and valued—not just in grand gestures, but in the small, everyday choices that say "You matter to me." Reversing neglect begins with awareness and intention. It's about making the deliberate decision to show up fully—for yourself and your partner. When both people commit to nurturing the bond, prioritizing each other, and addressing imbalances as they arise, the relationship not only survives—it deepens.

Love doesn't fade overnight. It fades when we stop tending to it.
And it comes alive again when we do.

Mistake 2:
An Attitude of Entitlement

An Attitude of Entitlement

Equality in a partnership lies in maintaining a sense of fairness, especially in status, rights, and opportunities. If you question your sense of entitlement, reflecting on your behavior within the relationship is crucial.

Financial Disparities: If you earn more than your partner, do you believe it entitles you to preferential treatment? Equality means making decisions together, not exerting dominance based on income.

Workload Imbalance: Assess whether you're sharing responsibilities in a balanced manner. If your partner is working long hours, it's essential to contribute more to home activities, ensuring equality.

Decision-Making: In an equal partnership, significant decisions should be made collaboratively. If one partner consistently dominates decision-making, it erodes equality and fosters resentment.

Maintaining an equal partnership requires fairness and mutual respect. It's not about the power dynamics or financial contributions; it's about acknowledging each other's unique skills and coming together to create a balanced life.

Acknowledgment and Affection: Cultivate a habit of expressing affection when you return home. Pay attention to your partner's day, especially during challenging times, and provide extra care when needed.

Shared Responsibilities: On good days, take the initiative to handle everything—from cooking to cleaning. Learn essential tasks if needed. Remember, money isn't the key to your partner's heart; active participation and support matter more.

Acknowledging Unique Skill Sets: Recognize and appreciate each other's strengths and skills. If one excels in finances and the other in household details, divide tasks based on individual strengths, making it a fair distribution of responsibilities.

Mutual Agreement: Discuss and agree on how to divide chores, finances, and other aspects of daily life. Be fair in assessing each task's time, ensuring an equal distribution.

Prioritizing Each Other: Even amid a busy schedule or personal hobbies, prioritize your partner. Remember that an equal partnership means putting your partner first and finding time for shared activities.

Ultimately, an equal partnership thrives on communication, mutual understanding, and a commitment to fairness. It's a collaborative effort to create a balanced and supportive relationship where both partners feel heard, respected, and cared for.

Equality in a partnership isn't about keeping score—it's about keeping pace with each other emotionally, mentally, and practically. It's a daily dance of give and take, led by mutual respect, clear communication, and shared values. When one partner feels unheard, unsupported, or overburdened, the balance begins to tip, and connection gives way to quiet discontent.

But when both partners commit to fairness—not perfection—something beautiful happens. The relationship becomes a safe, empowering space where each person can thrive, supported by a foundation of trust and genuine partnership.

True equality is found not in grand declarations, but in everyday choices: showing up, stepping in, and lifting each other up. When both partners prioritize each other and move through life as a team, love deepens, resentment fades, and the relationship becomes not just equal—but

extraordinary.

Mistake 3:
Setting False Expectations

Setting False Expectations

Consistently failing to follow through on commitments can profoundly impact a relationship, eroding trust and creating feelings of neglect. It's crucial to recognize the consequences of unfulfilled promises and work towards building a secure partnership.

Impact on Partner's Feelings: Unmet commitments breed doubt, resentment, and disappointment in your partner. It can make them feel left out, undervalued, and uncertain about the security of the relationship.

Health Consequences: The stress caused by broken promises can manifest in health issues for your partner, such as weight gain, depression, and a low self-image. Your actions directly affect their emotional well-being.

Self-Image and Motivation: Constant neglect can harm your partner's self-image, leading to a loss of motivation for self-care activities. They may feel unappreciated, aging, and less attractive, affecting their overall well-being.

Commit and Deliver: Make commitments and stick to them. Prioritize these commitments if you promise to complete tasks or be home at a specific time. Consistency in keeping promises builds trust and security.

Reduce Partner's Stress: Actively listen to your partner's concerns and sources of stress. Make it a priority to minimize their stress levels by fulfilling your promises and addressing the issues they find challenging.

Clean Track Record: Uphold a clean track record of fulfilling promises. A happy partner contributes to a strong and secure relationship. This security allows you to pursue personal activities without worrying about repercussions.

Building Goodwill: Completing tasks and fulfilling commitments accumulates goodwill. Think of it as an investment; the more goodwill you get, the more positive returns you receive regarding a grateful and content partner.

Addressing Complaints: Completing tasks on the honey-do list isn't about avoiding additional work but addressing persistent complaints. Removing the stickum notes of uncompleted tasks leads to a happier partner and a more harmonious home.

Immediate Action: Develop the habit of direct action when your partner needs help. Avoid procrastination and prioritize your partner's needs. This contributes to their happiness and allows them the freedom to pursue their desires.

In summary, a secure partnership is built on trust, consistency, and the fulfillment of commitments. Prioritize your partner's needs, create a positive track record, and address concerns promptly. Only when your partner's core needs are met can the relationship thrive and fulfill both partners' desires. Remember, transparency and active communication are essential; "don't ask, don't tell" is not a viable option in a partnership.

At the heart of every strong relationship is reliability—the quiet power of doing what you say you'll do. When you consistently show up, follow through, and take your partner's needs seriously, you build more than trust; you build emotional safety, stability, and long-term connection.

False expectations, no matter how unintentional, leave lasting emotional imprints. They create invisible cracks in the foundation of love, leading your partner to question your words, your priorities, and ultimately, the relationship itself.

But when you replace empty promises with consistent action, everything shifts. Your partner relaxes. Their defenses drop. Gratitude replaces frustration. And what you create together is not just a relationship—it's a sanctuary.

In the end, it's simple: mean what you say, say what you mean, and deliver with love. Because a promise kept is not just a task completed—it's a message that says, "You matter. I see you. I've got you."

38

Mistake 4:
Telling Lies and Keeping Secrets

Telling Lies and Keeping Secrets

Deception, whether in the form of white lies or more severe transgressions, can profoundly affect a relationship by undermining trust and instilling feelings of insecurity. Recognizing the diverse nature of lies and their consequences is pivotal for constructing and sustaining a foundation of trust in a partnership.

White Lies vs. Serious Lies: White lies are often employed to sidestep trouble or spare someone's feelings, while serious lies, such as addictions or leading a double life, carry significant consequences that can result in a breakdown of trust.

Privacy and Boundaries: Establishing clear boundaries concerning privacy and determining what can be shared with friends and family is crucial. Disclosing private information, particularly about one's intimate life, without mutual agreement can lead to breaches of trust. Respecting each other's privacy is essential to fostering a healthy relationship.

Differences in Lifestyles: Effective communication is vital if partners have differing lifestyles or social preferences. Understanding each other's needs and reaching agreements on rules and strategies can help prevent feelings of neglect or disconnection.

Exaggeration and Overinflation: Habitual exaggerating of achievements or creating larger-than-life stories can evolve into deception. Over time, partners may question the authenticity of statements, casting doubts about other aspects of honesty.

Technology and Intimacy: Excessive use of phones or social media during shared moments, like meals or bedtime, can negatively impact intimacy. Establishing rules, boundaries, and strategies for technology use is essential to maintain a sense of connection and intimacy in the relationship.

Honesty and Integrity: Acknowledge that even minor lies, white lies, or exaggerations can erode trust. A commitment to honesty and the readiness to admit mistakes, apologize, and seek forgiveness when necessary is essential.

Rebuilding Trust: White lies can lead to a breakdown of trust; once lost, rebuilding becomes a challenging process. Partners may become more vigilant, checking phones and emails or questioning whereabouts. Rebuilding trust necessitates openness, transparency, and a sustained commitment over time.

Being an Open Book: To rebuild trust, openness about actions and whereabouts is crucial, and giving your partner access to your phone and passwords can aid in the process. Understanding that regaining trust is a gradual journey may require forfeiting certain freedoms until trust is fully restored.

Commitment to Honesty: Honesty is the foundational pillar of a trusting partnership. While it may pose challenges, embracing truthfulness is essential for the purity and longevity of the relationship.

Conclusion: Maintaining a trusting partnership demands honesty, establishing clear boundaries, and mutual respect for each other's privacy. Rebuilding trust after lies, even seemingly minor ones, necessitates transparency, openness, and a sincere commitment to change. Always remember that honesty is the key to a healthy and lasting relationship

p

WHAT STAGE IS YOUR PARTNERSHIP

ADJUSTING

INCOMPATIBILITY

DISRESPECT

SELFISHNESS

Chapter 3:
Four Stages of Relationship Decline

Four Stages of Relationship Decline

Look inward before you point fingers.

In Chapter One, you learned about the four mistakes that can derail a partnership: neglecting or overlooking your partner, setting false expectations, feeling entitled, and engaging in lies and secrets. These mistakes can solidify into habits, leading to the four stages of survival: Adjusting, Selfishness, Disrespect, and Incompatibility.

I introduce two metaphors to illustrate how partners instinctively protect their sanity: "flipping the switch" and "building a brick wall." The switch metaphor represents partners disconnecting when they perceive unreasonable behavior, protecting their sanity from neglected responsibilities or constant complaints. The brick wall metaphor is the emotional distance partners create by building a wall, one brick at a time, in response to broken promises or unfulfilled commitments.

We'll later teach you how to encourage your partner to remove bricks and rebuild trust.

Stress and real-life issues in a relationship can lead to fighting and disconnection, impacting overall happiness. Even minor issues can become sources of annoyance and control during challenging times. Partners may feel taxed and out of control, contributing to relationship strain.

The good news is that your partner likely holds onto hope, wanting to believe they didn't make a mistake in choosing you. They hope that the emotional connection, though faded, can be rekindled.

"A perfect partnership is found between two imperfect people who refuse to give up on each other." n chapter one you learned about the four mistakes made to dereal a partnership. Neglecting or overlooking your partner, setting false expectations, feeling entitled, and engaging in lies and secrets can derail a relationship, fostering an environment of hurt and disappointment. Over time, these mistakes can solidify into habits that force your partner to shield themselves from potential harm and frustration. So a partner can over time change and kick in what I call the four stages for survivor. These four stages are Adjusting, Selfishness, Disrespect and Incompatability.

I use two metaphors or tools they use to keep the relationship going the first is what I call, "flipping the switch" and the second is "building a brick wall," I will illustrate how partners instinctively protect their sanity and shield against disappointment with these two tools.

The "switch" metaphor represents a protective mechanism your partner develops over time. It's triggered when they perceive your behavior as irrational, overwhelming, or emotionally exhausting. Whether it's due to repeated broken promises, neglected responsibilities, or constant complaints, they eventually "flip the switch" to preserve their own sanity. In this state, your words—no matter how loud or emotional—are reduced to background noise. They're not listening anymore. They've emotionally disconnected, not out of malice, but as a means of self-preservation.

The brick wall metaphorical is the wall a partner will build one brick at a time ever time a promises is broken or commitments are unfulfilled. The higher the wall, the less they rely on you to meet your obligations, creating emotional distance and disappointment. Later we will teach you how to get you partner to remove bricks and now add any.

Stress and real-life issues in a relationship can lead to fighting and disconnection, impacting overall happiness. When the relationship is thriving, certain bad habits may be tolerated, but even minor issues can become sources of annoyance and control during challenging times. Partners may feel taxed and out of control, contributing to relationship strain.

The good news is that your partner likely holds onto hope, wanting to believe they didn't make a mistake in choosing you. They hope that the emotional connection, though faded, can be rekindled.

A perfect partnership is found between two imperfect people
who refuse to give up on each other.

ADJUSTING

46

Stage 1:
Adjusting

In the adjusting stage of a relationship, your partner, sensing a lack of reliability in you, begins adapting their expectations and takes on responsibilities independently. While individual problems may not immediately threaten a relationship, persistent patterns of neglect or unfulfilled commitments can accumulate, evolving into more significant concerns over time.

In the beginning, my partner and I shared everything—responsibilities, decisions, and emotional connection. We were in sync. But over time, I started to notice a shift. I'd often promise to help out more, to be home on time, to show up in the ways my partner needed—but too often, I didn't follow through. At first, they would express their frustration, hoping I would change. But when things stayed the same, something in them began to change instead.

They stopped asking me for help. Instead of waiting for me to follow through, they just did it themselves. Instead of planning weekends around us, they started making their own plans. The emotional conversations grew fewer and far between. I didn't see it at the time, but they weren't angry—they were tired. Tired of hoping, tired of being disappointed. So they quietly adjusted.

And honestly, at first, I thought things had gotten easier. There were fewer arguments, less tension. But I didn't realize they had flipped the switch. They had stopped depending on me emotionally. They were still there physically—but emotionally, they had checked out.

It wasn't about punishing me. It was about protecting themselves.

By the time I noticed the distance, they had already built a rhythm without me. The connection hadn't disappeared overnight—it had slowly faded in the shadow of broken promises and unmet needs. And suddenly, I was no longer at the center of their life... I was on the outside, looking in.

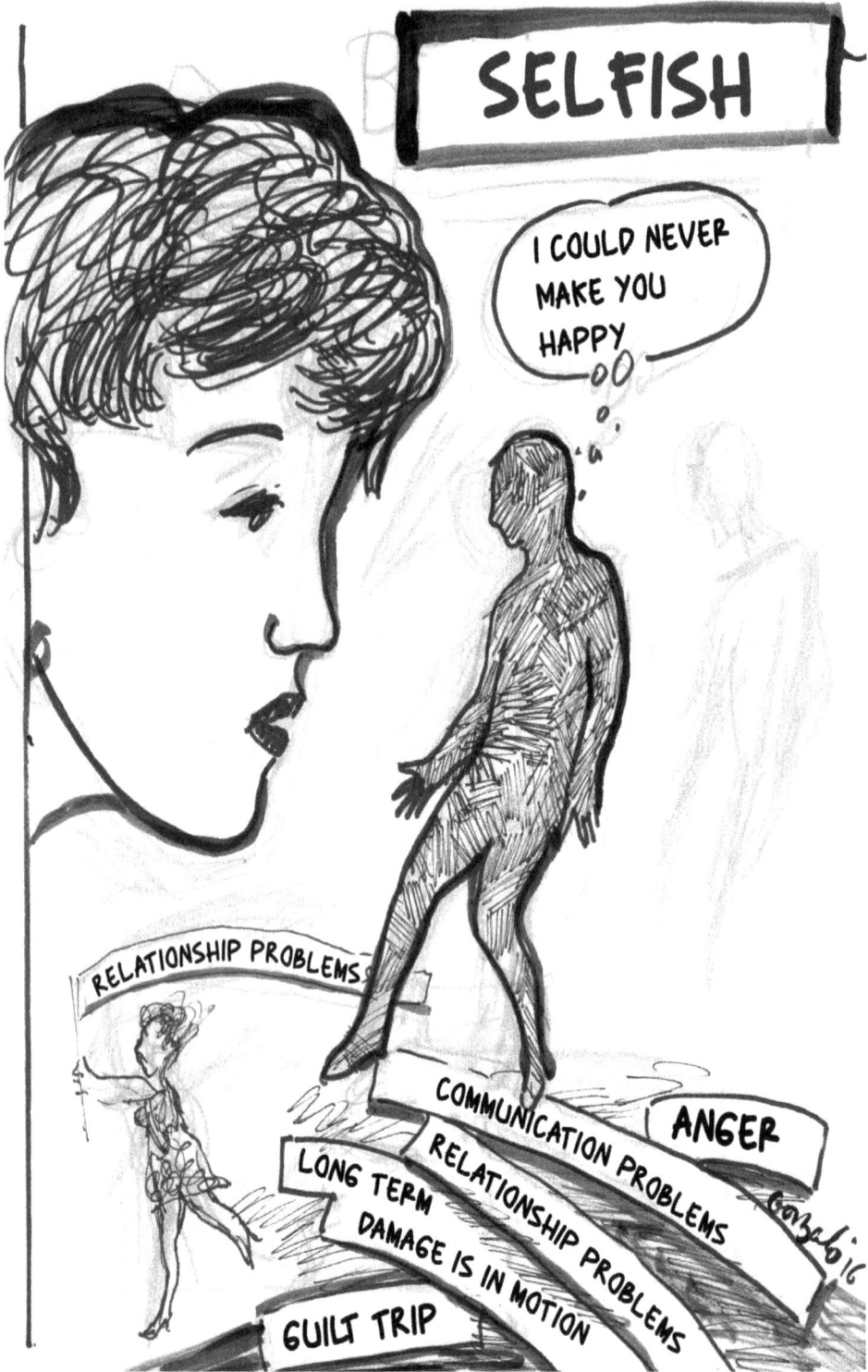

Stage 2:
Selfishness

The Selfishness Stage, often referred to as the "Everyone for Themselves Stage," is a phase marked by your struggling partner's attempts to assert control and rectify issues. Polite requests transform into demands accompanied by predetermined consequences, sometimes laced with ultimatums. This stage may leave you feeling incapable of satisfying your partner, encountering retaliatory statements like dictating holiday plans to underscore the repercussions of your actions.

At some point, I realized things with my partner had shifted again. The quiet adjustments they once made in silence turned into firm demands. What used to be polite requests—"Can you help more around the house?" or *"It would mean a lot if you showed up on time"—*became non-negotiable commands with consequences attached. "If you can't prioritize this family, don't expect me to change my plans for the holidays," they'd say. I started to feel like I was constantly walking on eggshells, unsure of what would set them off next.

When I tried to step up, it never seemed to be enough. If I cleaned the kitchen, I'd get a list of ten more things I didn't do. If I offered help or asked how to support them, I'd be met with silence—or worse, sarcasm. The emotional tone of our relationship had become unpredictable. One moment they were calm, the next, angry or withdrawn. I didn't know who I was coming home to.

Eventually, I started to check out. Not because I didn't care, but because I didn't know how to connect anymore without setting something off. I began avoiding certain conversations. I found reasons to stay busy. We both did. We were still under the same roof, still doing life—but emotionally, it felt like we were living separate lives.

This stage wasn't just about them being unreasonable—it was about both of us trying to survive in a space where communication had turned reactive, not connective. We were no longer working together. We were protecting ourselves from each other.

Stage 3:
Disrespect

The Disrespect Stage manifests through escalating arguments that turn ugly, marked by eye-rolling, name-calling, and yelling. In this stage, every spoken word is recorded, and the playback button has been activated, creating an atmosphere charged with anger that brings out the worst in both partners. Disrespectful interactions can inflict deep wounds in the relationship, making it challenging to climb out of the hole that forms.

During this stage, partners may engage in hurtful behaviors, including ridiculing each other during conflicts. An "I don't care" attitude often accompanies the decline in mutual respect, with partners becoming indifferent to addressing relationship issues, allowing problems to accumulate. Despite this, the fear of failure and the desire to regain control may drive efforts to salvage the relationship, especially when both parties recognize the need for change.

By the time we reached this stage, something in me had shifted—and not for the better. The warmth and patience that once defined our relationship were replaced by frustration, sarcasm, and a constant need to defend myself. Conversations with my partner weren't just arguments anymore—they were battles. Every discussion turned into a contest, and every word spoken seemed to be stored and later weaponized.

I remember one night clearly: I rolled my eyes at something my partner said, and they snapped. It escalated fast—name-calling, raised voices, and jabs that cut deeper than either of us admitted. We both said things we couldn't take back. It wasn't just about the dishes or the plans that fell through—it was about the resentment that had been building under the surface for far too long. We had started keeping score—not of wins, but of wounds. I could feel the distance growing, and worse, I could feel my respect fading. I stopped looking at my partner the way I used to. I stopped caring if they were happy or not. And I knew they had stopped caring too. We weren't cheating, but we were drifting—flirting with emotional boundaries, checking out mentally, occasionally fantasizing about how it might feel to be with someone who didn't feel like the enemy. It felt like we were living on opposite ends of a battlefield, each holding onto our pride while our connection lay in ruins between us.

INCOMPATIBLE
We cannot agree
On anything
You yell at me
All the time
I hate how you
treat me
You are just
a bad roommate
You
do not
respect
me
Why are
we even
together?

Stage 4:
Incompatibility

The incompatibility stage marks a critical point in the relationship where partners find it challenging to agree on anything, leading to a sense of bleakness. Mutual respect has crumbled, and the specter of incompatibility looms large. Navigating through this stage is a daunting task, requiring a glimmer of hope and a shared commitment to work through the underlying issues. It's a pivotal moment when the realization that "love is not enough.

By the time we reached this stage, it felt like we were just coexisting. My partner and I used to laugh at the same jokes, binge the same shows, and finish each other's sentences. Now, we couldn't even agree on what to eat for dinner. Every conversation felt like a negotiation—or worse, a trap. We weren't fighting constantly anymore… but that's only because we had both stopped trying. The silence between us was heavier than any argument we ever had.

I started spending more time at work, and when I was home, I found excuses to stay busy—working out, scrolling my phone, even texting with old friends just to feel something. My partner withdrew too, leaning on hobbies, long solo walks, and late nights in a different room. We stopped touching, stopped talking about the future. When we did speak, it was about logistics not love.

At one point, I caught myself wondering what it would feel like to be in a relationship where I didn't feel so alone. And I hated that thought. But the truth was, we weren't lovers anymore—we were roommates, moving through the motions, trying to avoid setting each other off.

Then one day, my partner said they were done. Not in anger, but in a quiet, exhausted voice that told me they had checked out long ago. And in that moment, everything hit me. The love I thought would always be there… wasn't. And suddenly, I was overwhelmed with regret—for every ignored conversation, every dismissive comment, every moment I thought we had more time. I realized too late that love isn't enough when respect, connection, and compatibility have eroded. And what hurt most was knowing that some of what broke us could have been fixed—if we had seen the signs earlier and truly tried.

PART 2:

Building a Strong Relationship Foundation

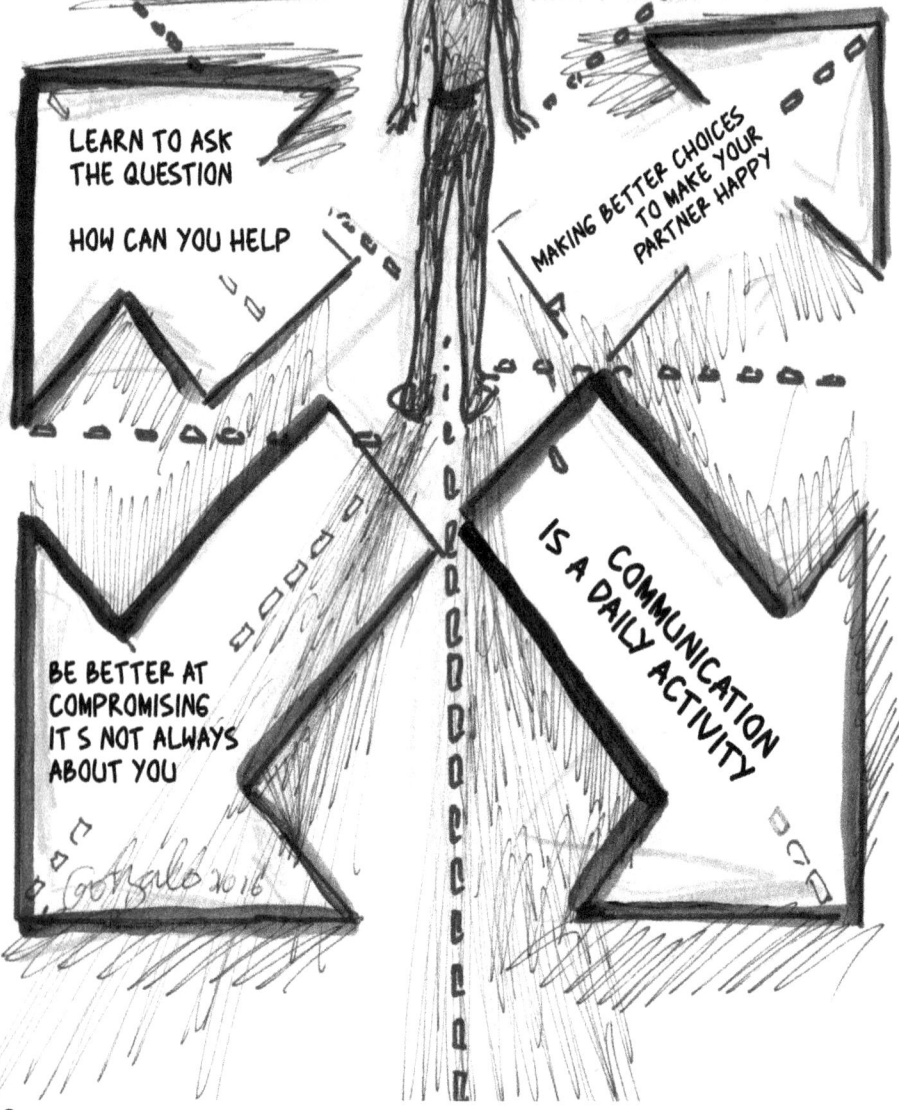

FOUR SKILLS FOR A HAPPY RELATIONSHIP

LEARN TO ASK THE QUESTION

HOW CAN YOU HELP

MAKING BETTER CHOICES TO MAKE YOUR PARTNER HAPPY

BE BETTER AT COMPROMISING IT S NOT ALWAYS ABOUT YOU

COMMUNICATION IS A DAILY ACTIVITY

Chapter 4:
Four Skills for a Happy Relationship

A partnership is a continuous project, and ongoing learning is key to significantly improving its quality. If you've faced challenges in your relationship, it may not be your fault; perhaps you were never taught the four critical ways to cultivate a healthy connection. Understanding and practicing these skills can alleviate stress and create a more harmonious partnership. Here are the four essential skills tailored to resonate with guys:

Skill 1: Ask the Question. You can't read your partner's mind, but staying attuned to their emotions lets you sense when something is amiss. Asking questions like, "Is there something I did wrong or can do better?" fosters strength and balance in the partnership. Remember, it's about understanding your partner's needs and working together to enhance the relationship.

Skill 2: Make Good Choices. When your partner requests something, ignoring or neglecting it disrupts the balance in the relationship. Making good choices involves honoring your partner's requests and participating in shared responsibilities. It's about being accountable for your actions and contributing positively to the partnership.

Skill 3: Compromise. A healthy partnership involves give-and-take. If you strongly advocate for a particular stance and your partner yields, be willing to compromise on another issue. Maintaining balance is crucial for mutual satisfaction. It's not about winning or losing but finding common ground that benefits both partners.

Skill 4: Communicate. Effective communication is the cornerstone of a successful partnership. Keeping your partner informed about decisions that impact both of you builds trust and prevents misunderstandings. Share your thoughts and listen actively to your partner's concerns. Communication is a two-way street that plays a vital role in fostering understanding.

Make your life mission to create a stress-free, happy partnership. Consistently apply the four skills and explore extra tools at the book's end for guidance. Your journey toward a healthier relationship continues with newfound knowledge and tools.

Skill 1:
Ask the Question

Questions serve as a valuable tool in fostering constructive communication within a relationship. Couples may need to truly understand each other's needs to fulfill perceived expectations. People are not mind readers, and assuming otherwise can lead to misunderstandings.

So ask bravely, listen fully, and respond with love. Because the truth is, every strong relationship is built not just on answers—but on the courage to ask the questions that matter most.

Here's a secret to maintaining a solid connection: Pay attention to signs of disconnection in your partner, such as a lack of communication, absence of laughter, or edginess, without an apparent reason. Instead of passively letting it slide, take a proactive approach by saying, "Do you have a minute? I want to ask a question. I want to improve and am clueless about what I did wrong. But, more importantly, I'd like to know how I can make it right." This opens the door for your partner to express their feelings, demonstrating your commitment to making better choices in the future.

Consider a scenario where one partner requires more alone time. Misinterpretation of this need can lead to feelings of neglect. Instead of jumping to conclusions, ask questions like, "Do you feel we have a balanced relationship?" or "Do you feel this partnership is equal?" Addressing the issue of trust is also crucial. Listen attentively to the responses and take notes to show genuine interest.

Asking questions allows your partner to vocalize their thoughts and feelings. The key is to focus on the core question behind every inquiry: "How can I be a better partner for you?" This approach encourages open communication and understanding, paving the way for a stronger and more fulfilling relationship.

The simple act of asking a question can be one of the most powerful tools in a relationship. It shows humility, emotional maturity, and a willingness to grow. Rather than assuming, reacting, or withdrawing, asking thoughtful questions invites your partner into a space of openness and connection. It tells them, "I care enough to understand, not just be right."

MAKING CHOICES

You said 15 minutes, and now it's a hour. why are you still working

i'll be with you all weekend

JUST ONE MORE CHANGE

Skill 2:
Make Good Choices
Every action is a choice.

In a relationship, every choice—big or small—sends a message. It says something about your priorities, your awareness, and your level of respect for your partner. Good choices don't just reflect wisdom; they reflect consideration—a conscious decision to honor the partnership, even when no one is watching.

Decision-making in a relationship can be challenging, as it involves considering your partner's needs and maintaining a balance between individual choices and shared decisions. When you were single, decisions were independent and had minimal impact on others. However, within a relationship, the quality of decision-making plays a crucial role in determining its success.

Prioritizing your partner's needs is essential for building a healthy partnership. It's important to recognize that every action is a choice, and decisions should be made with the relationship in mind. While some options can be made independently, making significant decisions without discussing them can lead to hurt feelings and strain the relationship.

Making good choices is not about perfection; it's about intentionality. It's about pausing to think, "How will this affect the person I love?" and being mature enough to choose what nurtures trust, connection, and growth. It's also about empowering your partner to make decisions, supporting their independence, and trusting that you're both striving toward the same goal—a strong, balanced, and meaningful life together.

The strongest relationships are built not just on love, but on thousands of thoughtful choices made with each other in mind. So choose wisely, choose kindly, and most of all—choose together.

Compromise

IT'S NOT ALWAYS ABOUT YOU

Compromise
Is all about your
partner having a
voice and an opinion
that you follow.
It's not always about
you.

Skill 3:
Compromise

In a healthy relationship, both people give—not because they have to, but because they want to. They recognize that love is not about winning, but about growing together. When compromise is practiced with honesty, empathy, and openness, it strengthens the bond, deepens trust, and creates a sense of shared purpose.

Practice this skill by putting your ego in check when making hardline decisions. Reassess whether insisting on your way is beneficial. Often, your partner's choice may be correct and even better. Embrace the idea that compromising doesn't mean weakness; it signifies strength and collaboration.

In relationships, disagreements are inevitable, but agreeing on how to handle them is essential—a form of love language. If conflicts arise, allow space for both partners to cool off before discussing the issue. If compromises feel more like sacrifices or an imbalance in efforts, it's crucial to reevaluate standards and boundaries to avoid falling into people-pleasing habits.

Learning the skill of compromise takes time, and it's essential to address issues before reaching a point of frustration. Reengaging with honesty and the willingness to admit when you're wrong can strengthen the foundation of a healthy relationship. Remember, it's okay to say, "You're right, I'm wrong."

Compromise is not about keeping score or losing battles—it's about choosing connection over control. It's a quiet act of love that says, "I value us more than I need to be right." When done with intention and mutual respect, compromise becomes a powerful way to show your partner that their needs, feelings, and voice truly matter.

So next time you find yourself at a crossroads, take a breath and ask: Is this about me, or is this about us?

Because often, the most powerful thing you can give in a relationship... is the willingness to meet halfway.

Skill 4:
Communicate

Effective communication is the cornerstone of building mutual respect in a relationship. Clear communication eliminates guesswork, avoids misunderstandings, and fosters trust, allowing partners to support each other and grow in love. In challenging conversations, practice active listening by repeating your partner's words to show understanding. Small gestures like eye contact, holding hands and nodding keep partners feeling like teammates rather than opponents.

During meaningful discussions, put away mobile phones and laptops, and consider using a "safe word" to take breaks when needed. Spending ten minutes daily letting your partner vent creates a positive communication channel. Avoid complacency, express yourself when things feel unfair, and be open to saying, "You're right, I'm wrong," if necessary.

While it's not your fault if you weren't taught the essentials of a healthy partnership, this knowledge removes any excuses moving forward.

Communication is not just about words—it's about presence, patience, and the willingness to understand before being understood. When we communicate with intention, we create a space where vulnerability feels safe, emotions feel heard, and love feels secure.

It's easy to talk, but real communication requires listening with your heart, not just your ears. It's choosing to lean in when things feel hard, and choosing connection over comfort when silence seems easier. Small gestures—eye contact, a soft touch, a sincere "I hear you"—can bridge even the widest emotional gaps.

You may not have been taught how to communicate in a healthy relationship, but now that you know, you have the power—and the responsibility—to do better. Because nothing builds or rebuilds a relationship faster than honest, kind, and consistent communication. So speak with love, listen with empathy, and never underestimate the healing power of a simple conversation shared between two people willing to grow.

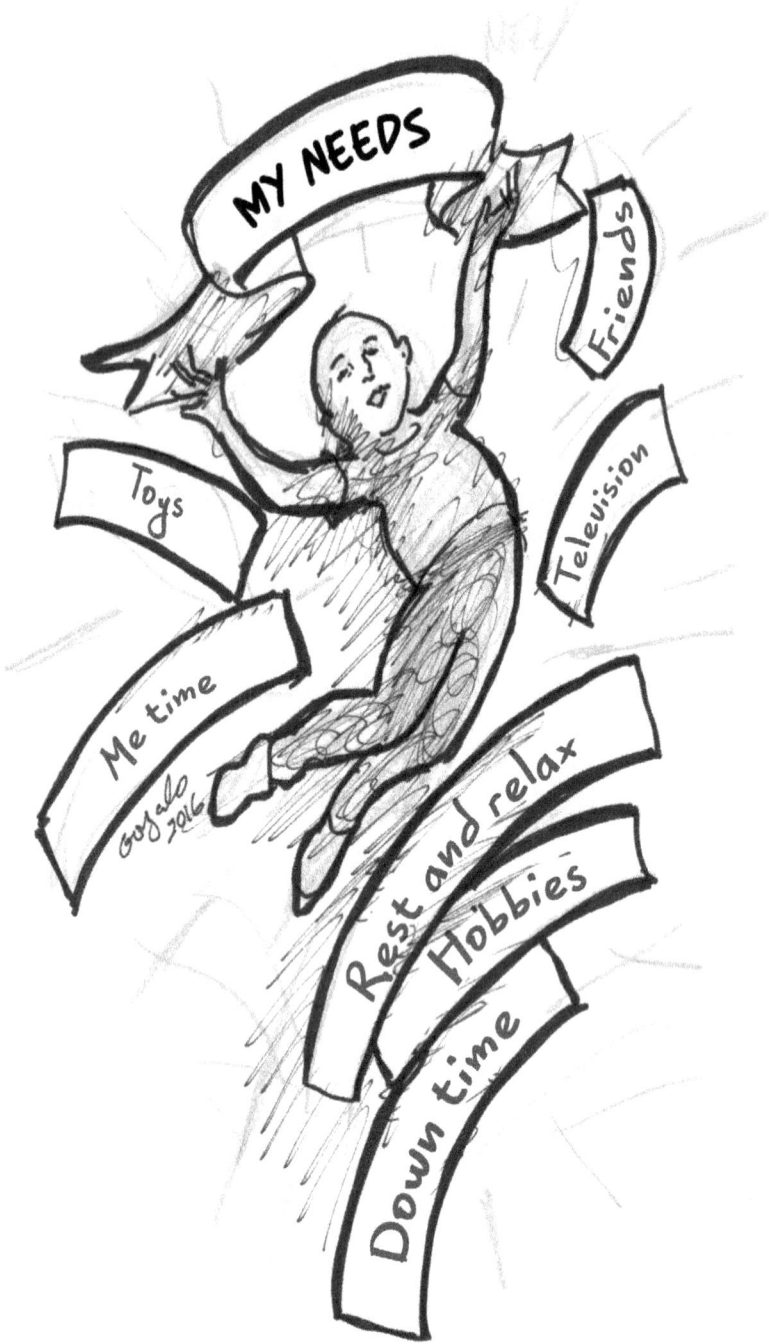

MY NEEDS

Friends

Toys

Television

Me time

Gigalo 2016

Rest and relax

Hobbies

Down time

Chapter 5:
Your Needs to Be Happy

Consider yourself the rock, the foundation of your relationship's bridge. This chapter explores the four needs your partner should honor for your happiness. Think of yourself as the cornerstone of the bridge, crucial for its strength.

Your partner's four needs, explored in the next chapter, act as pillars supporting the bridge. If your foundation is solid and you meet your partner's needs, you create a strong bridge, fostering mutual support.

Distinguish between needs and wants in your relationship. Needs are essential requirements, while wants are desires. While meeting your partner's needs is crucial, meeting your wants is equally necessary for a fulfilling life.

The goal is reciprocal support for needs and wants, creating a healthy partnership. Focus on necessities first, then communicate your wants to your partner. Remember, they have wants, too.

Life rocks when both partners' needs and wants are met, ensuring a healthy partnership. In the metaphor of a bridge, you are the foundation, and daily issues are the support beams that can shake the pillars. Explore these further in Chapter 6.

Now, let's delve into what makes you happy, addressing four basic human needs:

Need 1. LIKE
Need 2. DON'T LIKE
Need 3. SUCK AT
Need 4. HATE

Understanding and respecting these four needs pave the way to a simple truth: your happiness is ensured when acknowledged.

YOU KNOW WHAT YOU LIKE TO BE HAPPY

Need 1:
What I LIKE

The first essential need for your happiness is what you like in life. The LIKE need encompasses things that make life truly fulfilling. Life becomes vibrant and enjoyable when your partner respects and supports your preferences. Here are some critical aspects of the LIKE need:

Being Needed and Wanted: Feeling appreciated with compliments and affectionate gestures and knowing your partner truly values you.

Companionship: The desire for a fun, loving partner who doubles as your best friend—a person you can always be around and genuinely enjoy.

Competitiveness: The thrill of competition and winning, whether in games with friends or for your favorite team. It's an adrenaline rush to feel alive.

Fixing Things: The satisfaction of resolving issues, whether verbally or physically. Accomplishing tasks when acknowledged boosts your confidence,

Forgiving: Recognizing the importance of forgiveness as. It's crucial for moving past conflicts and focusing on more positive aspects of life.

Sex: Your sex life contributes to your overall well-being—physically, spiritually, and emotionally. It enhances your confidence and sense of vitality.

Thinking Big: Allowing yourself to dream big and envision future plans, career changes, or personal goals. Your partner by your side is critical.

Toys, Gadgets, Hobbies, or Sports: Engaging in mental relaxation is crtical and needed. These pursuits contribute to a sense of purpose and well-being.

Venting: The need to unwind, vent, and share your thoughts with your partner strengthens the connection, and validates a sense of care and love.

When your partner acknowledges and respects your needs, your life becomes complete with fun and happiness.

WHAT I DONT LIKE

CONSTANT COMPLAINING

Fighting

Being Wrong

Chores

Nagging

BEING WRONG

Heated Arguments
Reminded of Past

Being Trashed
Being Controled

SECRETS

Need 2:
What I Don't Like

The second essential need revolves around what you don't like. Just as your partner respects your preferences for what you enjoy, it's equally crucial for them to honor what you DON'T LIKE. Constantly being pushed to do things you dislike will trigger negative emotions like anger and resentment.

Here are common DON'T LIKE scenarios:
Being Trashed: Negative comments about your work or efforts can profoundly affect your self-esteem. Criticisms like "You did the job half-assed" or "I could have done it better" create a hostile atmosphere.

Chores: The aversion to chores is relatable, but avoiding them is not an excuse. Communicate with your partner about tasks you dislike and find a compromise to share the responsibilities.

Constant Complaints: Dealing with a partner who consistently complains can be draining. Try to understand the root of the complaints and adjust.

Heated Arguments: Disliking intense arguments and loss of control is natural. In such situations, disrespectful words may be spoken unintentionally. It's essential to find ways to manage conflicts calmly.

Nagging is irritating, and nobody likes it. If you're facing constant nagging, reflect on whether your actions or unfulfilled commitments are contributing.

Racquet Ball Effect: The back-and-forth of blame or recalling past promises can strain the relationship. Avoiding this "Racquet Ball Effect" requires open communication and addressing issues constructively.

Bringing up past problems alongside current ones sucks. Focus on resolving current issues without dragging the baggage from the past.

White Lying: Telling white lies to avoid conflict or unreasonable requests is common but harmful practice. It's critical to find a solution together.

Remember, your partner's opinion holds significant value, and understand respecting each other's dislikes contribute to a health relationship.

WHAT I SSUCK at

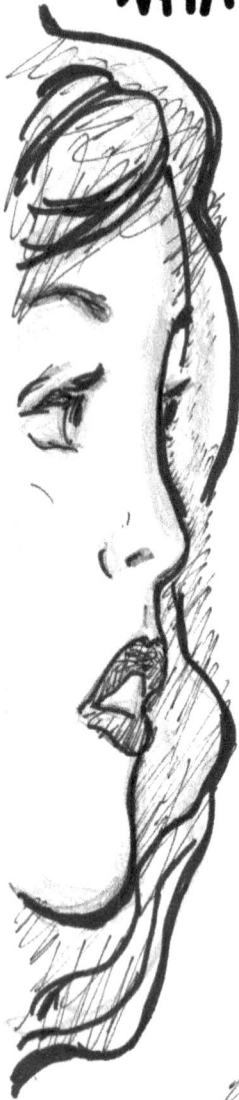

Asking for Help

Doing activities we don't want to do

Admitting you're Wrong

Completing Tasks

Details

Long Conversations

Being accountable

Chores

72

Need 3:
What I Suck At

The third crucial need centers on what you SUCK AT. Like DON'T LIKEs, your partner must respect these areas to ensure your happiness. Being forced to engage in activities you're not adept at triggers childhood insecurities, recalling times when you felt inadequate.

Here are ordinary SUCK AT situations that might resonate with you:
Admitting You're Wrong: Acknowledging mistakes can be challenging, especially if you pride yourself on being the most intelligent person in the room. It's embarrassing when your partner points out your errors, and hearing "I was wrong" feels degrading.

Asking for Help: While resources like YouTube can assist with challenging tasks, your pride might hinder you from seeking help. The reluctance to ask for assistance stems from a perception that you suck at it.

Completing Tasks: Unless a task promises a significant reward, it may not be a priority. Similar to dogs expecting treats for good behavior, the motivation to complete tasks might be tied to rewards.

Details: Dealing with intricate details might seem time-consuming. In a world of instant gratification, focusing on short, quick, and straightforward approaches becomes the norm, and handling details is an area where you may feel you suck.

Long Conversations: The SUCK AT response is triggered when faced with lengthy conversations. Attention spans may be short, and the mind tends to multitask, making it challenging to engage in extended discussions.

Keeping Opinions to Yourself: Expressing opinions is inevitable. If you have a viewpoint, it's likely to surface one way or another.

Navigating these areas with understanding and respect from your partner contributes to a healthier and more fulfilling relationship

WHAT I HATE

Begging for Sex

Being Controlled

Being Manipulated

Picking up after
yourself

To hear the words,
we need to talk

Being Told What To Do

Being Yelled At

"WE NEED
TO TALK"

GONZALO
2016

74

Need 4:
What I Hate

The fourth and final need is centered around what you HATE, and respecting this need is crucial for your happiness in the relationship. When compelled to engage in activities you hate, it triggers the HATE need, leading to anger and resentment.

Here are everyday HATE situations that you might relate to:

Begging for Sex: The need to pray for sex can strongly trigger the HATE need. Feeling cut off or having to plead for intimacy can make you feel abnormal and miserable. It challenges your pride, humility, and self-worth.

Being Controlled: When your partner dominates decision-making, doesn't listen, and places unbalanced expectations without shared responsibilities, you feel controlled. It creates a sense of incompetence when you perceive you have no say.

Being Manipulated: No one likes being manipulated, and this aversion is at the core of the HATE need. The feeling of being outsmarted implies a lack of control over the situation, triggering the HATE need.

Picking Up After Yourself: Some partners may object to picking up after you with the phrase, "I'm not your mother." This objection can be sensitive, implying a reliance on maternal care for basic needs.

We Need to Talk: "We need to talk" can instill fear in a partner's heart, as it often precedes serious discussions or confrontations.

Reflecting on these categories—LIKE, DON'T LIKE, SUCK AT, and HATE—allows you to identify and share your needs with your partner. The goal is mutual acknowledgment of each other's needs, paving the way to address potential disconnects in the relationship. Understanding and managing your partner's needs are crucial to fostering a deeper connection.

YOUR PARTNER'S NEEDS

Balance
Equality
Security
Trust

This Is What Your Partner Needs For A Great Relationship

This is Were The Disconnect Begins

If **WOMEN** Didn't exist all The **MONEY** in the world would have **NO MEANING**

Chapter 6:
Your Partner's Needs to Be Happy

You become the best possible partner when you assist your partner in fulfilling their needs. Do you desire happiness, love, respect, and friendship in your relationship? This chapter holds the secret sauce to a great partnership, unveiling the factors that often lead to relationship failures—unmet partner needs.

Your partner's four needs support your bridge, ensuring a solid foundation when fulfilled. The acronym BEST encapsulates these pillars:

Balance

Equality

Security

Trust

Your responsibility is to safeguard these pillars, honoring and respecting your partner's needs. This involves supporting and understanding the Four Mistakes that may have impacted your partner and your relationship. Recognizing your role as the foundation is crucial, as the foundation must settle first. Understanding why your partner's needs haven't been met is essential for a happy partnership.

Modifying behaviors becomes imperative for a positive change. Remember, your needs will only be met if your partner's needs are addressed. Aligning with the goal of a happy partnership is critical. Each pillar is influenced by daily issues; positivity and support maintain them, while negativity and unresponsiveness can cause damage.

Cracks in the pillars manifest as nagging or persistent complaints. Ignoring these signals may lead to a deteriorating relationship. Repairing each pillar requires attention, specific tools, and skills. It's a gradual process, akin to inspecting a neglected bridge. Deep cracks may take time, but there's always hope with consistent efforts and the right tools.

Hope is a valuable gift for your partner. Without it, the relationship might not endure. In the upcoming chapters, delve into your partner's four needs, assess the damage, and explore ways to strengthen each pillar. Reflect on past experiences to identify where you have overlooked your partner's needs.

BALANCE

PHONE
Turn off phone at dinner

TEAMWORK

I Now Understand That I Have Not Been Meeting Your Needs So That You Can Be Happy

Gonzalo

Quality time is critical Sports & Hobbies need balance

Don't fix your partner's problems be a good listener

Need/Pillar 1:
Balance

Uneven pillars create an unstable bridge, and an unbalanced relationship is similarly at risk of collapsing. Achieving balance involves supporting your partner in various daily activities, from household chores to kids. Recognizing when your partner needs assistance, without them having to ask, is critical to maintaining balance and fixing cracks in the Balance pillar.

Daily issues affecting relationship balance include:
Family
Friends
Habits
Health
Hobbies & Sports
Kids
Venting
Work

Additionally, more complex issues, referred to as "baggage,"
Addiction
Depression
Trauma
Wants vs Needs

A balanced relationship thrives on teamwork during challenging situations. Finding a steady rhythm creates balance, equality, security, and trust. Stepping up when your partner is overwhelmed or facing difficulties is crucial. Taking the initiative without being asked fosters a balanced relationship. The give-and-take dynamic, symbolized by Taoism's yin and yang philosophy, It emphasizes that two halves together create something whole.

Ask yourself: What impedes achieving this level of balance in your partnership? Activities like excessive involvement in hobbies or sports, listening to sports commentators, or being consumed by personal interests without dedicating time to your partner can disrupt balance.

EQUALITY

Your Partner's Voice Is Heard

SHARED RESPONSABILITY

Mutual Decision

Open Communication

80

Need/Pillar 2:
Equality

In a relationship, equality entails respecting your partner's thoughts, opinions, and suggestions to ensure they have a voice. It involves mutual acknowledgment and appreciation for each other's contributions. The key to fixing cracks in the equality pillar is to let go the feelings of entitlement.

Daily issues affecting relationship equality include:
Appreciation
Arguments
Avoiding Conflict
Beliefs
Disrespect
Selfishness
Responsibilities
Voice

Additionally, more complex issues, referred to as "baggage,"
Co-dependency
Commitment
Keeping Score
Resentment

Inequality, the opposite of equality, is reflected in behaviors like interrupting, talking over your partner, imposing control over decisions, making them walk on pins and needles, expressing anger, and dismissing their understanding. Both partners should embrace cooperative behavior, setting aside ego.

For example, if your partner typically makes dinner and isn't home one night, step into the kitchen and cook instead of questioning or opting for TV dinners. With equal contributions, this cooperative approach signifies equality, partnership, and love.

Equality stresses mutual respect, valuing your partner's needs and voice equally. Disagreements should be handled without interruptions, condescension, or yelling. Anticipating your partner's needs before expression is a goal that deepens your connection, making you the partner they can't stop talking about and solidifying a lasting bond. 81

SECURITY

Going out to dinner
phone in hand
Not really
Connecting

Going to a holiday party and
leaving your partner is not
really connecting

82

Need/Pillar 3:
Security

A secure relationship allows partners to be authentic, communicate openly, and feel emotionally safe. Insecurity can lead to complications like doubt, confusion, jealousy, and sadness. To fix security pillar cracks, avoid setting false expectations, as discussed in Chapter 2.

Daily issues affecting relationship security include:
Emotional support
Feeling loved
Finances
Jealousy
Manipulation
Stress
Temper
Weight

Additionally, more complex issues, referred to as "baggage,"
Abuse
Financial Secrets
Forgiveness
Self-Esteem

Ensure one of your life goals is to make your partner feel secure. Actions like flirting with others or being wasteful with money can trigger your partner's need for security. In a secure relationship, partners empower each other to act independently while maintaining mental and emotional balance.

Take responsibility for setting a tone of insecurity by avoiding negative comments, insults, or dissatisfaction. Your behavior plays a crucial role in either empowering or degrading your partner's sense of security. During disagreements, treat your partner with respect, avoiding public degradation.

Recognize that financial security contributes to your partner's overall sense of security. When making financial decisions, navigate compromises and communication to address your partner's security needs, even if it conflicts with your own desires. Support your partner in making their dreams come true, fostering a secure partnership.

Need/Pillar 4:
Trust

Trust is the foundation of a successful relationship, and its absence results in an unstable partnership. Consider the trust pillar as weight-bearing, impacting all pillars simultaneously when damaged. With irrecoverable deception, the bridge may not support even a feather. To repair trust, eliminate lies and secrets, as discussed in Chapter 2.

Daily issues affecting relationship trust include:
Boundaries
Integrity
Intimacy
Lifestyle
Relationship Dynamics
Second Guessing
Technology
White Lies

Additionally, more complex issues, referred to as "baggage,"
Abandonment
Deception
Disconnection
Double Life

Trust, like respect, must be mutual, with both partners believing in each other. When trust is violated, winning it back can be challenging. Some relationships start with trust and test it over time, while others gradually build trust. Partners may conduct "White Lie Tests" to check honesty, leading to additional scrutiny if failed. Being an open book, sharing everything can rebuild trust and restore freedom in the relationship.

A crucial lesson is to avoid actions you wouldn't do with your partner present, preventing boundary violations and cheating suspicions. Transparency, such as allowing access to phones and emails, can provide peace of mind and restore trust. Completing tasks, whether plumbing or remodeling, also builds trust, while unfinished projects can erode it. Consistently delivering on promises and overachieving can strengthen trust in the partnership. Without trust, the foundation of a meaningful relationship is compromised.

PART 3:

RESET TO GET
YOUR PARTNERSHIP BACK

DAILY TOOLS FOR RELATIONSHIP BALANCE

Our partner wall is used to protect them from getting hurt

Our tool box needs to contain the tools necessary to break down

only when there is trust does our partenr start to remove the bricks one at a time

the walls between us and our partner

Gonzalo

Daily Tools to Restore Your Relationship

Now that you've arrived at this point, it's time to begin the reset—an intentional, thoughtful process to repair and strengthen your relationship.

Before diving into the tools, take a moment for yourself. Give yourself permission to pause and reset emotionally. Whether it's a run, a walk in nature, a moment of stillness, or quiet meditation, releasing stress and clearing your mind will help you approach this process with clarity, empathy, and renewed energy.

This chapter offers practical, daily tools designed to help you address and restore the four pillars your partner depends on: trust, support, respect, and emotional safety. With real-life examples and actionable steps, you'll find ways to recognize common issues and shift into healthier habits—one day, one moment at a time.

Work together with your partner to explore these tools. Invite honest feedback and remain open to growth. If difficult or painful comments arise, it's okay to take a step back. Revisit them with care when emotions have settled. Healing often stirs up past pain, but facing it with grace and patience is the first step toward a stronger, more connected partnership.

Approach this process one issue at a time. As you begin to repair the cracks in your partner's pillars, you'll start rebuilding not only trust—but a resilient bridge that carries both of you forward.

For deeper insights, more examples, and guided support, visit www.youarerightiamwrong.com.

BALANCE
HONEY, IF YOU'RE WORKING LATE I'LL HAVE DINNER READY FOR YOU
HONEY, I will drop off TH KIDS
HONEY, I'LL GO GET THE GROCERIES
2016

CHAPTER 7:
BALANCE PILLAR
8 Daily Tools for Relationship Balance

Family

Familial Influence and Boundary Crossings: Navigating Challenges in Partnership

Family is where life begins, and navigating the complexities of family dynamics is crucial for a harmonious partnership. "Navigating Family Challenges, Drama and Demands: Builds Harmony in Your Relationship" you need to discuss the influence and boundaries that family members are crossings.

The dynamics become challenging when various family members, from grandparents to siblings, feel entitled to express their opinions and influence your partnership without invitation. Imposing values and viewpoints disrupts harmony, and imbalance arises when family members overstep their boundaries.

Even joyous occasions like holidays can bring stress. Balancing tasks and deciding which family to spend holidays with can be overwhelming. Trying to please everyone may resurrect childhood issues, creating tension in your partnership.

Sibling rivalries, with roles like the golden child or black sheep, can lead to ongoing conflicts in adulthood, undermining harmony with your partner.

Financial matters involving family can strain the partnership, especially if there needs to be more agreement with your partner.
Maintaining an open-door policy with family or succumbing to guilt-driven pressure on weekends and holidays poses challenges.

Respecting each other's needs, finding compromises, and addressing manipulation are essential. Firmly holding your ground against guilt-tripping siblings is crucial to protecting your partner.

Family Tool: Partner First

Struggling with family boundary issues, difficulty saying no to their demands, or feeling manipulated by guilt can strain your partnership. If your partner perceives excessive time spent with family or finds their demands unreasonable, resentment can build.

To overcome these challenges, adopting the "Partner First" approach is crucial.

It's time to assert yourself with your family, prioritizing your partner's needs above all else. While it may initially hurt their feelings, establishing healthy boundaries is vital for your partnership's well-being. Balancing family demands with work, friends, and personal activities is essential to prevent your partner from feeling neglected.

Recognize that your family's expectations may seem unreasonable, and trying to please everyone is impossible. Embracing the "Partner First" mindset allows you to shift the focus onto your partner, making decisions as a team to navigate family influence.

Sharing family conversations and decisions with your partner integrates them into your family dynamic. However, respect their privacy and avoid sharing sensitive information without consent to maintain trust.

To set boundaries, detach from the constant need for approval and stick to your decisions. If family members cross boundaries, hold them accountable by implementing consequences, such as a three-day timeout. This emphasizes that their behavior is unacceptable.

Successful implementation is evident when your family stops laying guilt trips on you. Never blame your partner for relationship shortcomings when discussing these issues

Friends

*You can't write a story together
if you're not on the same page.*

Friendship plays a significant role in our lives, impacting our mental well-being and influencing the choices we make. Friends have the ability to ignite the part of the brain associated with positive feelings, help us cope with stress, and contribute to better decision-making. They serve as a support system, keeping us grounded and boosting our morale.

When it comes to relationships, a partner appreciates friends who respect boundaries, exhibit reasonableness, and add an element of fun. These qualities make it easier for a partner to accept and enjoy your friendships. However, friends can also pose challenges if they display neediness, make unreasonable demands, or act selfishly. Such behaviors may lead a partner to develop a dislike for them.

The impact of friends on a relationship is significant due to the bond and trust that has developed over the years. Friends can inadvertently make a partner question your judgment, especially in challenging decisions. Opting for a friend's advice over your partner's can create trouble, as it may undermine the foundation of trust in your relationship.

Sharing too much personal information, or airing your relationship's "dirty laundry," with friends can be risky. While seeking advice from friends is natural, involving too many people can be detrimental, especially when dealing with private matters. It's essential to maintain a balance and be cautious about sharing sensitive details that should remain within the confines of your partnership.

Competing with your partner's best friends is not the solution. Instead, the key is acceptance and alignment with your partner on how friendships should coexist within the relationship. However, if friendships become imbalanced or cross boundaries, it's crucial to acknowledge and address the issue with your partner.

Admitting mistakes and saying, "You're where right, and I'm wrong," can contribute to open communication and the resolution of any concerns, fostering a healthy balance between your relationship and friendships.

94

Friends Tool : Same Page

The dynamics between a partner and friends can sometimes lead to feelings of competition, resentment, and potential drama within a relationship.

The Same Page tool can be utilized to address these issues:

Identify and Address Competing Priorities: Resentment can arise if a partner dislikes or does not accept friends. The Same Page tool encourages open communication about how friends fit into the partnership, clarifying expectations regarding time spent with friends and involvement. Both partners should acknowledge the importance of friendships and work towards a compromise on any conflicting issues.

Communication and Conflict Resolution: When conflicts arise, it's crucial to communicate openly. The Same Page tool emphasizes discussing issues privately, understanding the reasons behind actions, and agreeing on ways to prevent similar occurrences by addressing concerns constructively.

Establishing Clear Rules: Setting rules with friends is a critical aspect of the Same Page tool. On issues such as friends being overtoo much, concerns about excessive drinking when with those friends, lateness, or changes in behavior. It's your responsibility to keep friends in check. and find a balance.

Handling Disrespectful Friends: If friends disrespect a partner, shut it down. Friends should not have a say in the relationship, and any disrespect toward your partner is critical for you to shut that down.

Prioritize Partner First: In times of overload or when a partner feels neglected, it's essential to prioritize the partner over friends. The Same Page tool encourages fairness in allocating time and emphasizes the concept of "Partner First." Real friends will understand and respect boundaries.

By applying the Same Page tool and incorporating effective communication, rule-setting, and prioritization, individuals can navigate the complexities of balancing friendships and relationships, creating a harmonious environment where both partners feel valued and respected.

Habits

*Habits are like a comfortable bed—
easy to get into but hard to get out of.*

Indeed, let's delve into the concept of bad habits, differentiate between action and attitude habits, and explore their impact on relationships. Additionally, I'll share some thoughts on addressing and owning up to these habits.

Action Bad Habits: Noticeable behaviors, from grooming lapses to thoughtless actions, can accumulate frustration. Excessive screen time, including phone use and social media, also falls into this category.

Attitude Bad Habits: Approaching the relationship with neglect, excuses, or a constant need to be right creates negativity. Subtle behaviors, like ignoring a partner's voice during meals, contribute to an overall hostile atmosphere.

Recognition and Impact: Acknowledge that these habits may have been present from the start. Minor issues can transform into significant tension if addressed. If a habit bothered your partner initially, it likely still does.

Ownership and Communication: Take ownership if bad habits become problematic. Saying "You're right, I'm wrong" shows a commitment to address concerns. Open communication allows partners to express feelings without judgment.

Continuous Improvement: Relationships require ongoing effort. Identify and acknowledge bad habits, working together to establish healthier patterns. This involves setting boundaries, sharing responsibilities, and finding compromises for mutual respect and ongoing positive change.

In summary, addressing bad habits involves recognizing their existence, understanding their impact, and working to improve. Taking responsibility for one's actions and attitudes fosters a healthier relationship built on mutual respect and ongoing commitment to positive change.

Habits Tool: Come On

Changing Habits for a Stronger Partnership

Identify and Acknowledge:

Begin by listing the habits that bother your partner. Recognize the importance of change and commit to improvement.

The Come On Tool: Embrace the "Come On" tool, encouraging self-reflection: "You're smart. Figure it out. Identify what bothers your partner and make the effort to change."

Skills from Chapter 4: Apply skills like compromise and letting go. Utilize the 21-Day Rule to eliminate habits causing frustration.

21-Day Rule Implementation: Employ the 21-Day Rule—new behaviors become the norm after consistent application. Use reminders, stickers, or calendar notices to stay on track. Overcome temptations with practical strategies, such as putting the phone away during dinner.

Consistency and Reset: Acknowledge that bad habits may resurface during busy or tired moments. Put them in check and reset as needed. Consistent focus over time will lead to habit elimination.

Reward System: Involve your partner in a rewarding system. Discuss and agree on rewards, fostering motivation for positive change.

Attitude-Based Habits: Address attitude-based habits using the Same Page tool. Understand the underlying reasons and strive for balance in the partnership.

Replace with Good Habits: Create a list of positive habits to replace the undesirable ones. Communicate intentions to your partner. Consistently practicing good habits will naturally overshadow the negative ones.

By committing to change, utilizing effective tools, and incorporating positive habits, you can strengthen your partnership, fostering a more harmonious and supportive relationship.

Health

Strengthening Partnership
in the Face of Illness

The presence of illness can disrupt the balance in a relationship, especially when it's self-inflicted. Unhealthy lifestyle choices strain partnerships, making them feel like incompatible roommates. If your partner communicates health concerns and you persist with detrimental behaviors, it's unfair to the relationship.

In Self-Inflicted Illness: Unfair to the Partnership: Unhealthy choices like smoking, excessive drinking, poor diet, and chronic stress negatively impact growth and happiness.
Accountability: It becomes unfair when concerns are communicated, but detrimental behaviors persist, affecting the relationship.

Chronic Illness: True Self Emerges: Facing a chronic illness reveals strength and resilience, requiring skill-building and guidance.
Partners' Unique Approaches: Both partners bring their thoughts and processes, impacting the partnership during challenging times.

Navigating Emotions: Emotional and Logical Handling: Chronic illness challenges emotions and logic simultaneously, lacking quick fixes.
Be a Supportive Partner: Approach the situation with empathy, understanding, and patience. Seek help when feeling lost.

Conclusion: Facing a chronic illness is a journey with no easy solutions. Partners, whether directly affected or supporting, navigate emotions and logic differently. Being a fantastic partner involves strength, support, and a willingness to seek help. Remember, both individuals contribute to the partnership's resilience during challenging times.

Health Tool: Own It

When health issues arise, taking ownership and overcoming challenges together is crucial. If health problems are self-inflicted, recognizing their impact is essential. The solution is to "Own It."

For Self-Inflicted Health Issues: Impact on Partnership: Acknowledge that neglecting health affects your partner and the partnership.

Mutual Growth: True partnership involves growth, happiness, and mutual support. Changes are necessary for a healthy relationship.

Communication and Support: Actively communicate and support your partner dealing with health issues. Proactively assist with medication, meals, and chores.

Utilize the 21-Day Rule: For self-inflicted health issues, apply the 21-day Rule and seek support from friends and a reliable system. Shift focus towards reclaiming a partnership free from dependencies.

Facing Chronic Illness: Solid Support: Both partners should be supportive during illness. Strive to be on the same page, compromise and respecting each other's decisions. Align Emotions and Logic: Emotions can cloud decision-making, so strive to align emotions and logic for effective decision-making.

Maintaining Balance: Active Care: Actively care for each other and avoid assigning passive roles. Set boundaries around caregiving and ensure reciprocity.Embrace the "New Normal": Focus on being a couple beyond the illness. Life is a shared journey; embrace the "new normal" together.

Express Emotions: Share Emotions: Allow expression of various emotions, supporting each other emotionally. Expand your support network with those who understand your situation.

Harness Willpower for Positive Change: Take Ownership: Commit to positive change for your health or your partner's. Communicate openly and admit when necessary. True partnership means facing challenges together with strength and unity.

Hobbies & Sports

We interrupt this partnership
to bring you football season.

Hobbies and sports are essential outlets—they're great for mental health, stress relief, and personal enjoyment. But like anything else, when taken to the extreme, they can quietly hijack your relationship.

When hobbies or sports dominate your time and attention, your partner may start to feel like they're competing with another love in your life. And let's be honest—no one wants to feel like second place to a team, a tee time, or a fantasy football draft.

So, ask yourself honestly: Are you striking a balance?
If your free time is completely consumed by stats, scores, or solo pursuits, while shared time with your partner keeps getting pushed aside, the scales are tipped. And it's worse when you can recall every detail about your favorite player's salary—but forget your anniversary, your kid's recital, or your partner's birthday. That's not just offside—it's messed up.

If your mood swings with the scoreboard, and your emotional availability is more in tune with the game than with your partner's needs, something has to change. Relationships shouldn't have to compete with your pastimes.

Meanwhile, who's holding things together while you're locked into your next big fantasy league move? Who's doing the errands, handling the family logistics, folding laundry? If the answer is always your partner—that's not a partnership. That's a solo act with a support crew.

Hobbies and sports only become a problem when they cross boundaries. And if you've crossed that line, the best move isn't a defensive play—it's ownership. A simple, sincere:
"You're right. I'm wrong."

That's how you get back in the game—the one that really matters

Hobbies and Sports Tool: Really

The Really tool is a practical approach to balancing your hobbies and sports with your partner's needs, emphasizing multitasking, time management, and compromise. If you genuinely want to enjoy your hobbies, you must fulfill your committed responsibilities first. This tool encourages a give-and-take approach, ensuring that both partners' needs are considered.

Here's how to apply the Really tool: Prioritize Partner's Needs: Before indulging in your hobbies or sports, ensure your partner's needs are met. If tasks from the honey-do list are pending, prioritize and complete them first.

Communication and Planning: Ask your partner what is critical and create a comprehensive list of tasks. Plan and organize the tasks, considering the tools and materials needed. Effective time management and planning.

Complete Projects: Start and finish the projects you undertake. While multitasking is acceptable, ensure all initiated tasks are completed before taking on new ones. Seek your partner's input upon completion.

Reward System: Implement a reward system. Request one hour of game time for every two hours spent on honey-do lists. This serves as both a time management strategy and a reward for completing responsibilities.

Incremental Progress: Break down the honey-do list into manageable sections. Tackle ten easy items, each taking less than 30 minutes to complete. Create a time schedule for each item, striving to improve your scheduling with each set of tasks.

Review and Redo: Have your partner review the completed tasks. If there are issues, be open to feedback and avoid arguments. Redo the functions until they are done right, as incomplete or poorly done tasks don't count.

Consistency and Improvement: Consistently apply the Really tool over time. As you complete the entire list, you'll notice a positive shift in your partner's attitude, allowing you more playtime.

By mastering the Really tool, you can strike a balance between your hobbies and responsibilities, earning love, friendship, and trust and fostering a genuine partnership with your significant other.

Kids

If I ever go missing, just ask my kids.
They know how to find me wherever I'm hiding.

Raising kids brings immense joy but also challenges that impact your partnership. Alignment and teamwork are crucial, as it takes a village to raise a child.

Priority on Partnership: Balanced Focus: Kids should not be the sole focus. Prioritize your partner Well-being Chain: It's important that both partners prioritize each other's well-being, the children naturally benefit.

Equal Participation in Parenting: Tag Team Effort: Recognize that parenting is a joint responsibility. Avoiding Imbalances: Ensure both partners share the load.

Setting Healthy Boundaries: Avoiding Manipulation: Children may manipulate; consistency is key. Both partners should uphold shared boundaries to prevent behavioral issues.

Intimacy and Boundaries: Allowing kids in the bed regularly blurs boundaries. Preserve intimacy by setting clear limits.

Open Communication and Decision-Making: Shared Decision-Making: Communicate openly and make decisions together. Conflicts arise if one parent allows choices without agreement, undermining the partnership.

Acknowledging Weaknesses in Parenting: Admitting Mistakes: Emphasize the importance of admitting when wrong.

Prioritizing Partnership: Healthy Communication: Navigate complexities with open communication, shared decision-making, and setting boundaries. Preserving Relationship Strength: Prioritize your partnership to preserve the strength and happiness of your relationship amidst the challenges of raising kids.

Kids Tool: OMG

Setting boundaries, establishing rules, and creating dedicated private time is essential in navigating parenthood. Utilize the OMG tool to make informed choices and maintain balance in your partnership. Acknowledge the need for mutual support and recognize that handling everything alone is unrealistic.

Business Partnership Approach: Identify Skill Sets: and define responsibilities Regular Meetings: to discuss progress, and issues, with a plan of attact.
Set clear Boundaries: and rules, providing support when difficulties arise.

Prioritizing Communication: Find a balance between managing daily logistics and dedicat time for meaningful discussions.
Discuss crucial matters like discipline and child development

Active Support: Reducing Partner's Stress: Support each other to minimize stress. Prioritizing Well-being: to benefit both partners.

Maintaining Humor: Overcoming Challenges with Laughter: Maintain a good sense of humor, Regular Date Nights: Family outings are enjoyable, but regular date nights.

Spontaneous Intimacy: Significance of Spontaneity: Don't overlook spontaneous intimacy.

Overall Practices for a Strong Partnership: Reduce stress by actively supporting each other. Prioritize your partner's well-being to benefit both partners. Maintain a Sense of Humor: Overcome challenges with laughter. Regular Date Nights: Schedule regular date nights for intimate connection. Spontaneous Intimacy: Embrace the significance of unexpected moments.

Incorporating these practices will strengthen your partnership, help you navigate parenting challenges, and bring joy to your shared journey.

Venting

Ten minutes a day,
will keep the doctor away

The Importance of Venting in a Healthy Partnership

Venting is crucial to maintaining a healthy partnership, providing a safe space for your partner to release stress and tension. Allowing your partner 10 minutes to vent when they come home fosters a sense of connection and prevents potential problems.

Benefits of Venting: Venting allows your partner to open up about complex issues, reducing anxiety and stress. Addressing frustrations through venting contributes to a more balanced and harmonious partnership.

Distinguishing Venting from Complaining: It's essential to distinguish between venting and complaining, as unresolved complaints breed negativity. Striking a balance in addressing problems and seeking resolutions is critical.

Forms of Venting: Venting, in various forms like rants or text messages, acts as a pressure valve, releasing negative energy. Be mindful of how your partner receives venting messages. Unloading anger in a harmful manner is not venting but bullying.

Preventing Negative Emotions: Holding frustrations inside intensifies negative emotions, affecting mood and potentially changing personality. Venting prevents the buildup of resentment, anxiety, and anger that can explode if left unchecked.

Boundaries in Venting: Venting should never cross boundaries. Disrespectful behavior or manipulation undermines a healthy partnership. Maintain a positive and supportive environment through empathy, understanding, and respectful communication

Venting Tool: Ten Minute

The Power of the Ten-Minute Daily Tool for Connection

The Ten-Minute Daily Tool is a potent method to nurture connection in your partnership. By dedicating a brief yet focused time to actively listen to your partner vent, you demonstrate care and strengthen the bond of love and happiness. This skill set is essential for effective communication.

Implementing the Ten-Minute Tool: Investment in Happiness: Devote ten minutes daily to actively listen to your partner vent, creating a stress-free and loving environment.

Evening Routine: Imagine coming home, sharing a glass of wine, and conversing while your partner vents. It's an investment in meeting each other's needs.

Building Listening Skills: Authentic Listening: Develop the skill of truly listening as trust builds, allowing your partner to share inner thoughts comfortably.

Handling Vulnerabilities: Handle your partner's vulnerabilities carefully, avoiding judgment and negative comments during venting.

Improving Communication: Avoiding Negative Responses: Refrain from negative comments or one-liners during your partner's venting, preventing hurt and resentment.

Expressing Frustrations Positively: Wait for your turn to speak frustrations positively and respectfully, using "I" language and taking responsibility for your feelings.

Considerate Venting: Respecting Timing: Ask if it's a good time for your partner to vent, respecting their readiness and avoiding attacks or blame. Offering Support: Inquire how you can help or make changes to ease their burden and enhance the relationship. Be considerate in your approach.

Work

You should not look for happiness through work alone. Because work without a partner is loneliness.

The impact of work habits on relationships is a crucial aspect to consider. Here's a closer look at key points:

Workaholic Tendencies: Spending excessive hours at the office or consistently venting about work can strain your relationship. It's natural to discuss both positive and negative aspects of work, but constant complaints may wear thin on your partner over time.

Prioritizing Work Over Relationship: Assess whether you prioritize work over shared activities with your partner. Opting out of joint activities or bringing work stress home can create undue pressure on the relationship.

Strain on Relationship: Extended work hours, frequent weekends at the office, or bringing work home may strain the relationship. Difficulty in separating work and personal life can lead to unintentional discussions about work dominating conversations.

Communication Breakdown: Lack of varied topics in conversations beyond work may indicate a problem. If your partner expresses resentment toward your work or suggests you quit, it can manifest in other areas, leading to impatience and irritability.

Impact on Emotional Well-being: Bringing work stress home may result in unintended conflicts with your partner. New arguments about unrelated matters may emerge, and potential add stress on the relationship.

Acknowledging Work Boundaries: If work starts encroaching on personal boundaries, owning up to it is crucial. Recognizing the impact on your partner and admitting, "You're right, I'm wrong," shows accountability and a willingness to address the issue.

In summary, achieving a healthy balance between work and relationship is vital. Recognizing the signs of imbalance, being open to communication, and making conscious efforts to prioritize the relationship contribute to a harmonious and fulfilling partnership.

Work Tool: Keep Your Word

Achieving work-life balance can be challenging, especially when work provides a sense of purpose and accomplishment.

Sense of Purpose and Accomplishment: Work can be fulfilling, providing a sense of purpose and accomplishment that feeds the ego.

Integrity and Trustworthiness: The Keep Your Word tool reflects integrity, commitment, and trustworthiness in the partnership.

Start by focusing on a simple yet impactful aspect: keeping your word on when you'll be home or let your partner know if there is a change.

Time Management Strategies: Use alarms on your work calendar, smartphone, or watch to stay on track. If time management is challenging, enlist your partner's help by having them give you a call to remind you.

Boundary Setting: Establish clear boundaries with work colleagues regarding non-emergency calls after specific hours. If work tasks spill into personal time, find alternative solutions, such as waking up early to complete them.

Communication during Work Crunch: If your job has cyclical crunch times, communicate openly with your partner about the situation. Ensure mutual understanding of both short- and long-term goals and share any changes in plans promptly.

Making Up for Lost Time: Use the Keep Your Word tool to make up for lost time with your partner in alternative ways. Adjust your schedule, such as going to work early or staying late on another day, to prioritize commitments.

Mindset Shift: Applying the Keep Your Word tool prompts a shift from a work-centric mindset to building a positive relationship. Recognize that your partner needs your presence and attention, fostering a healthier and more balanced approach to both work and personal life.

Incorporating the Keep Your Word tool into your routine not only strengthens your commitment to personal relationships but also encourages a mindful approach to work, potentially leading to reduced stress and increased productivity.

BALANCE PILLAR

Addiction

Depression

Trauma

Wants vs Needs

Baggage Issue
Tools to Repair
The Balance Pillar

Unresolved problems that one or both partners
bring into the relationship.

Addiction

Addressing addictions in a relationship is like steering through a challenging course—it affects both partners. While recognizing our own addictive tendencies is critical, it's equally vital to grasp how these habits impact our partner and the relationship.

Ask yourself: Is my addiction fair to my partner? Despite seeming personal, addictions have consequences that ripple beyond the individual. When your partner or family is unintentionally caught in its web, it becomes a shared concern. Openly discuss your addiction with your partner, mainly if it affects them financially. Their feelings matter, and if they're uncomfortable, baggage needs attention.

Addiction often craves privacy, thriving in secrecy. Some think it's a personal matter, but in a partnership, well-being is intertwined. Your partner can voice concerns because it directly affects the relationship. Ignoring their perspective undermines the partnership, risking it becoming a mere roommate scenario.
Addictions trigger emotional changes, impacting the relationship's dynamics. Expecting your partner to stay out of it creates an environment of insecurity. Walking on eggshells isn't a sustainable way to maintain a partnership.

Recognize that addictions harm trust, stability, and emotional well-being. Both partners must actively address and resolve addiction issues. Seeking professional help or support groups can guide recovery. Open communication, empathy, and a shared commitment to overcoming addiction rebuild the partnership's foundation.

Remember, overcoming addiction is a journey. Actively working on it, being receptive to your partner, and seeking help lead to a brighter future for yourself and your partnership.

Addiction Tool: Willpower

Addiction doesn't just affect one person—it affects the entire partnership. But so does recovery. Choosing to confront your addiction with honesty and willpower isn't just a personal victory—it's a powerful act of love. It tells your partner, "I see the damage, and I'm willing to do the work to repair it."

Willpower isn't about being perfect—it's about being consistent, vulnerable, and committed to change. When you allow your partner in—when you lean on their support, share your struggles, and celebrate your progress—you invite connection back into your relationship. You prove that trust can be rebuilt, one truthful moment at a time.

Your courage to face addiction head-on can become the turning point not only in your life, but in the life of your partnership. Remember, you are not alone. With honesty, support, and willpower, healing is possible. And love can not only survive—it can grow stronger through the fire.

Confronting addictions is a complex challenge for both the individual and their partner. It's crucial to recognize that your partner may feel overwhelmed and unsure of how to support you, and witnessing your struggle might leave them feeling helpless. Despite the belief of being in control, addictions can spiral out of control, creating a distance between you and your loved ones.

Understanding that your partner's concerns are valid is essential. If they express genuine worry about the unhealthy level of your addiction, face it head-on and address it honestly. Take their concerns seriously, viewing them as an opportunity to reevaluate your situation and make positive changes. Willpower becomes a guiding force in this journey of change. Be honest with yourself, acknowledge the loss of control, and recognize how your addiction negatively impacts your life and partnership. With your partner's support, tap into your inner strength and commit to overcoming your addiction. Share your progress, challenges, and victories openly with your partner, fostering a sense of unity.

Your partner wishes to see you succeed and lead a healthy, fulfilling life. Embrace their support, allowing them to be a source of strength during this challenging time. By addressing your addiction with honesty, courage, and the power of will, you can rebuild trust, strengthen your partnership, and embark on a journey of healing and growth together.

Depression

Depression can be emotionally taxing; partners should foster open communication. Expressing feelings, concerns, and needs on both sides contributes to a supportive environment. If necessary, couples therapy or support groups can offer additional tools for navigating through the challenges.

Establishing boundaries and self-care practices becomes crucial in managing depression's impact on the partnership. Both individuals need to prioritize their mental health, recognizing that a healthy relationship relies on the well-being of each partner. Encouraging each other to engage in activities that bring joy, implementing stress-relief techniques, and creating a positive and understanding atmosphere contribute to a more resilient partnership.

Depression should not be a barrier to maintaining a fulfilling relationship. Partners can collaboratively work towards solutions, respecting each other's needs and boundaries. With proactive communication, empathy, and a shared commitment to well-being, a partnership can endure and thrive despite the challenges posed by depression. Seeking professional guidance and maintaining a positive outlook on the journey are essential components of this joint effort.

Depression may cast a heavy shadow, but it doesn't have to eclipse the love and connection within a partnership. When both partners commit to open communication, empathy, and mutual care, even the darkest days can be navigated together.

Healing is not a solo journey—it's a shared path. It's about checking in, showing up, and creating space for honesty without judgment. It's about offering support, but also knowing when to step back and protect your own well-being. Through patience, understanding, and a commitment to growth, couples can emerge stronger and more connected.

Remember, depression is not a weakness—it's a challenge. And together, with compassion and courage, you can face it head-on and build a relationship rooted in resilience, respect, and unwavering support.

Depression Tool: It's Real

Supporting a partner dealing with depression is a vital and compassionate contribution to a healthy partnership. Here are key steps you can take:

Recognize the Signs: Be aware of signs of depression and encourage your partner to reflect on their emotions, thoughts, and behaviors.

Create Open Communication: Establish a safe space for open and honest conversations about depression. Encourage your partner to express their feelings, concerns, and experiences related to their mental health.

Emphasize Professional Help: Stress the importance of seeking professional help. Provide guidance and resources to support them in finding suitable mental health professionals or treatment options.

Build Resilience: Help your partner build strength by encouraging healthy coping mechanisms, self-care practices, and stress-management techniques. Support their well-being by identifying activities that bring them joy.

Express Love and Support: Consistently show love and support. Offer reassurance, understanding, and empathy as your partner navigates their journey through depression. Remind them of your unwavering presence.

Encourage Acceptance of Help: Motivate your partner to be open to assistance from others, whether mental health professionals, support groups, or trusted friends and family. Clarify that seeking help is a sign of strength.

Promote Living Fully: Encourage engagement in fulfilling activities. Support the setting of realistic goals and steps towards achieving them, even amid depression.

Integrating the IT'S REAL tool into your support system provides a structured framework for addressing depression and finding pathways to a more fulfilling life.

Remember, your role is to be a supportive presence, listen empathetically, and aid in navigating the journey toward healing and recovery. Together, you can cultivate a stronger and more resilient partnership that thrives despite the challenges posed by depression.

Trauma

Trauma is a profound and transformative experience that can cast a lasting shadow on an individual's life. It's crucial to recognize that your partner may carry the weight of past traumas that still impact them, sometimes without conscious awareness. Triggers can unexpectedly activate trauma responses, causing emotional distress and difficulty coping.

Your partner's trauma has fundamentally shaped their life, altering their innocence and fortifying parts of their soul as a protective measure. Trauma can emerge from various sources and manifest in diverse forms, be it physical, verbal, or experiential. Understanding that trauma profoundly affects both individuals in a relationship is essential.

Navigating the effects of trauma demands a compassionate and empathetic approach. Establishing a safe space for open conversations is vital. Encourage your partner to share their experiences without judgment. Trauma is a deeply personal journey, and each person may have a unique perspective. Validate their feelings and offer support as they work through the impact of past experiences.

Sibling dynamics and family roles significantly contribute to how trauma manifests. Like being the golden child or the favorite, family rankings can shape self-perception and behavior. Acknowledging these dynamics is crucial in understanding how they may have contributed to your partner's trauma.

Trauma can manifest in various symptoms, affecting self-esteem, confidence, and the ability to pursue certain activities. It may lead to deep-rooted fears of inadequacy, perfectionism, or the inability to set boundaries—often replaying unresolved childhood roles in adult relationships."

Trauma Tool: I Got You

Healing from trauma is an ongoing process, and each step forward is a testament to their courage and determination. Embrace the positive changes you witness and encourage a mindset of growth and self-discovery.
Nurturing Intimacy and Connection:
Foster intimacy and connection within your partnership.
As your partner heals, prioritize moments of closeness and emotional connection.
Share activities that bring joy and create positive memories together.
Cultivate a sense of safety and love that strengthens the bond between you.
Intimacy can be a powerful healing aspect, fostering a deeper connection and understanding.

Reflecting on Your Own Role Reflect on your role in the healing process. Be aware of your own feelings, reactions, and boundaries. Seek support for yourself to navigate the emotional challenges of supporting a partner through trauma. Recognize the importance of maintaining your well-being to be a strong and supportive presence in your partner's life.

Building a Future Together Envision a future built on mutual growth, healing, and shared experiences. As you both embark on this healing journey, set goals and aspirations for the future. Cultivate a vision of a partnership that continues to evolve positively, marked by resilience, love, and a shared commitment to each other's well-being.

Incorporating the "I GOT YOU" Tool Consistently apply the "I GOT YOU" tool in your relationship. Use it as a foundation for communication, understanding, and support. Reassure your partner that you are there for them unconditionally, fostering an environment of trust and security. The "I GOT YOU" approach can be a guiding principle as you navigate the complexities of healing from trauma together.

Remember that healing from trauma is a shared journey that requires ongoing commitment, compassion, and understanding. By creating a safe and supportive environment, respecting boundaries, seeking additional support when needed, and embracing resilience and growth, you can contribute to a partnership that thrives despite past challenges. You can build a future marked by healing, connection, and shared strength.

Wants Vs Needs

In a scenario where your partner prioritizes showcasing a luxurious lifestyle through high-end purchases, extravagant getaways, and costly hobbies to project an image of success while you emphasize financial stability, sticking to a budget, and prioritizing practical expenses, significant challenges arise in your relationship.

This dynamic creates financial strain as your partner's extravagant spending leads to mounting debts, missed bill payments, and economic instability. Managing shared finances, you make sacrifices to address the aftermath of this financial mismanagement.
Witnessing your partner's neglect of financial responsibilities and disregard for overspending consequences may lead to resentment. The resulting financial stress and imbalance in the partnership can cause frustration, disappointment, and an erosion of trust.

Communication breakdowns become prevalent as attempts to address financial implications and responsible spending are met with defensiveness or dismissal from your partner. This dynamic impedes productive conversations about shared goals and establishing a solid financial foundation.

The persistent financial strain takes an emotional toll, causing anxiety and worry about instability due to your partner's spending habits. The stress of managing finances and ongoing tension in the relationship contribute to a lack of intimacy, emotional connection, and overall dissatisfaction.

To address these challenges, open and honest communication is essential. Both partners should feel safe expressing their concerns, needs, and goals without fear of judgment. Creating a shared financial plan, setting boundaries around spending, and possibly seeking guidance from a financial counselor can help rebuild trust and restore balance in the relationship.

Wants Vs Needs Tool: Put This in Check

Let's begin with open and honest conversations about our financial situation, sharing our concerns without judgment. This will allow us to better understand each other and find supportive ways to address these challenges.

To make a meaningful change, we must explore why we must keep up with others and the resulting feelings of inadequacy. This may involve self-reflection and empathy to understand the societal pressures, self-esteem issues, or desires for validation that drive these behaviors.

Let's work together to define our values and priorities, shifting our focus from material possessions to things that align with our true desires and bring long-term happiness. Setting meaningful goals based on these values will guide us toward a more fulfilling life.

I'm committed to supporting you in developing financial literacy skills. We can learn effective budgeting techniques, saving strategies, and ways to live within our means. We can enjoy life responsibly by creating a balanced budget that considers our needs and aspirations.

Mindful spending is a practice we can incorporate into our lives. Before making impulsive purchases, let's pause and evaluate if they align with our values and contribute to long-term satisfaction. Introducing a waiting period for non-essential purchases will give us time to reflect and make thoughtful decisions.
If, despite our efforts, changing spending habits proves challenging, seeking professional help is a proactive step. A financial advisor or therapist can offer tailored guidance to address deeper emotional issues or behavioral patterns.

I have confidence in our ability to make positive changes over time. Let's support each other on this journey, celebrating every small step toward healthier financial habits and a stronger sense of self-worth. Together, we can create a better future and build a solid foundation for our relationship.

Chapter 8:
Daily Tools for Relationship Equality

Appreciation

If you don't show appreciation when they deserve it, they'll stop doing the things you appreciate.

Failing to acknowledge and appreciate your partner's efforts can make them feel undervalued and may result in them stopping the positive actions you once valued.

Everyone desires appreciation, especially from their loved ones, as it is crucial to partner satisfaction. Partners who express daily appreciation for small and significant gestures tend to cultivate a culture of gratitude in their relationship. However, there are times when life's demands, such as work, health issues, or stress, can lead to a lapse in showing appreciation. Daily tasks become routine, and partners may overlook the importance of expressing gratitude.

A lack of appreciation in a relationship can foster resentment and create an unfair dynamic. It's not about grand gestures for every little thing, but a simple thank you goes a long way. When partners feel taken for granted, the shift from willingly caring for each other to an expectation of care can breed resentment.

Indicators that a lack of appreciation is impacting your relationship include the absence of expressions of gratitude, your partner not seeking your advice or opinions, making plans without involving you, unequal sharing of responsibilities, neglecting special occasions, lack of romantic efforts, infidelity, failure to inquire about your day or consider your feelings, and making decisions without consulting you for family events or bringing friends over without asking.

Not demonstrating appreciation can convey a sense of taking each other for granted. If you realize you've overlooked the importance of showing daily appreciation, it's essential to acknowledge it and say, "You're right; I'm wrong."

Appreciation Tool: I'm an Idiot

Appreciating your partner is crucial for a thriving relationship. If you need more clarification about how much you understand each other, create lists of daily contributions, such as chores, cooking, earning money, and other responsibilities. Compare the lists to ensure fairness.

If your partner bears more, acknowledge it and activate the "I'm an Idiot" tool to express gratitude and commit to doing your fair share.

Make an effort to show love and affection daily. Begin with small gestures like bringing coffee in bed or sharing a heartfelt kiss.

Leave love notes in unexpected places, such as the car dashboard or bathroom mirror. The power of a sincere, spontaneous expression of love is huge. Express gratitude with thoughtful gifts, plan surprise date nights, and remember special occasions like birthdays and Valentine's Day.

"Thank you" is a simple yet underused way of showing appreciation. If you're not pulling your weight, admit it and express gratitude to your partner. Demonstrate love through small gestures like leaving sweet notes or initiating unexpected phone calls. Support your partner by taking on responsibilities, allowing them time to unwind, or handling household tasks.

Incorporate Yes Days into your routine, where partners say "yes" to each other's requests on designated days. Yes Day enriches the partnership by satisfying your partner's wants and creating a deeper connection.

The power of a sincere, spontaneous expression of love can brighten your partner's Day and keep the spark alive in your relationship.

Consider taking a proactive approach to alleviate your partner's stress. Step up by saying, "I got this," and offer them a few hours of uninterrupted time to relax. Take care of daily tasks like shopping, cooking, and helping with the kids' homework, allowing your partner to unwind and feel supported.

Remember, expressing gratitude doesn't have to be grand; even small, consistent acts of appreciation contribute to a healthier relationship.

Arguments

Would you rather be right or would you rather be happy?

Consider asking your partner's opinion on significant matters this week and genuinely listen, incorporating their perspective where possible. Dedicate each night to letting your partner vent without interruptions or judgments. Experiment with a "Yes Day," saying "yes" to everything your partner desires. If your partner tends to invalidate your feelings during disagreements, it not only hurts but also jeopardizes the health of your long-term relationship.

In any relationship, occasional fights and heated debates are regular. However, when these escalate into full-blown arguments, the situation can quickly spiral out of control. Blaming each other or resorting to malicious comments is unhealthy and detrimental to the long-term well-being of the relationship.

Arguments about the division of responsibilities and daily chores are common. Addressing these issues constructively without using them as ammunition against your partner is crucial. Financial disagreements, especially when one partner is a spendthrift and the other is frugal, can strain the relationship, especially if funds are tight. Money-related conflicts often top the list of reasons for separation, indicating a misalignment in financial values.

Disputes involving friends and family can be emotionally charged, affecting individuals differently. Differences in opinion about the involvement of friends or family in your life can lead to problems. Overcoming jealousy takes time, and fighting over it may create significant challenges and crossing boundaries. In such cases, acknowledging and admitting when you're wrong can be a positive step toward resolution.

Tool For Arguments: I'm Sorry

Apologizing sincerely with an "I'm sorry" can go a long way in healing the disconnection and hurt caused by arguments. The apology is not an admission of being wrong but an acknowledgment of not being on the same page.

Reflect on the importance of having a partner who genuinely wants you around. Excessive arguing may lead to your partner desiring less time together. Ask yourself if you tend to argue too much.

Avoid believing you always have the correct answers, which implies viewing your partner as always wrong. Acknowledge that there can be multiple approaches to a task and consider the question: Would you rather be right or happy? Learning to stop and breathe before insisting on your way is valuable.

In times of anger, respond with calmness to prevent escalating tensions. If a conversation gets heated, express the need for time to calm down and continue the discussion rationally. Avoid arguing in public, as it can be humiliating and inappropriate. Establish private communication for negative matters.

Choose your battles wisely, approaching issues with a mindset of give and take. Avoid making sweeping statements like "you always" or "never" during arguments. Take a step back, consider your partner's perspective, and be willing to let go of issues that don't significantly impact your values.

While pride has its merits, excessive pride can harm relationships. Leave your ego behind, connect with your partner humbly and respectfully, and prioritize love and care over the urge to be correct.

Maintain confidentiality in arguments, letting the words spoken during a fight stay there. Give yourself breathing room before revisiting a disagreement to avoid talking in circles. Use the "I'm Sorry" tool to approach conversations and work toward a resolution.

Avoid Conflict

Tit for tat
leaves both partners feeling flat

Conflict is an inevitable part of any relationship and serves to adjust expectations and fortify the partnership. Handling conflicts constructively is crucial for the well-being of the relationship. Resolving conflicts leads to a deeper understanding of your partner, and finding mutually agreeable solutions is critical. Conversely, if conflicts persist without resolution, it can create an imbalance in the partnership and become problematic.

In the course of spending significant time together, disagreements are bound to happen. These disagreements can span various topics, from personal beliefs and career choices to parenting styles or differences in religious or political views. Recognizing that differences of opinion are average is essential. The crucial factor is how the partnership navigates these differences, with respect being the linchpin. Lack of respect becomes a red flag.

Sometimes, your partner may choose indirect ways to express their grievances instead of direct communication. This might manifest as condescending remarks, underlying hostility, or displaying a moody and pouty demeanor without addressing the core issue.

Partners may also avoid discussing problems by quickly changing the topic or being evasive. Indirect expressions of anger lack constructiveness as they need to offer clear guidance on responding, leaving the targeted person unsure of how to address the issue. Statements attacking your partner's character can significantly harm the relationship. While avoiding conflict to spare your partner's feelings might seem well-intentioned, it's not conducive to the long-term health of the partnership and can lead to resentment.

Steering clear of conflict can trespass boundaries and impede the relationship's growth. Remember the significance of acknowledging when your partner is right and admitting when you are wrong. Open and respectful communication tackles conflicts head-on and sustains a healthy partnership.

Avoiding Conflict Tool: Even Playing Field Method

Do you find yourself sidestepping conflict because it seems easier or out of fear of losing an argument? Are you harboring resentment because you feel unable to voice your opinions? Does your communication style lean towards withdrawal and shutting down? Do you suppress your emotions, thinking your voice doesn't matter? Then the Even Playing Field is your tool.

Many individuals seek to avoid negative interactions in their relationships, hoping to bypass dwelling on their shortcomings or mistakes. However, common conflict avoidance can erode intimacy and satisfaction and breed resentment. Ignoring unresolved conflicts creates distance and resentment.

Conflict avoidance often stems from sensitive topics triggering solid emotions, including past issues or disagreements on how certain matters were handled. While the natural inclination might be to change the subject or evade the conflict altogether, addressing the issue head-on is crucial; avoidance won't make the conflict magically disappear.

Approached constructively, arguments can foster empathy and provide insight into your partner's perspective, enabling open and honest communication about thoughts and feelings. Feeling overwhelmed and resorting to withdrawal when your partner wants to discuss their emotions is detrimental to the partnership. The Even Playing Field tool emphasizes developing practical communication skills.

Reducing stonewalling involves learning to communicate without accusations and judgments. Accusing your partner often leads to defensiveness, shutdown, and withdrawal. Strive to communicate without putting your partner on the defensive, understanding that disagreements are expected and compromise is essential for true equality.

During heated arguments, instead of checking out, ask your partner how you can work together to resolve the problem. Recognize avoiding conflicts due to feeling emotionally flooded can hurt your relationship. The key is be open and honest. The avoidance tactic of refusing to consider your partner's perspective often leads to emotional disconnection. To reduce conflict, learn to show vulnerability and communicate openly and honestly. Making repairs after an argument turns disagreements into a stronger partnership.

Beliefs

The best feeling in the world
is being wanted for who you are.

Navigating differences in beliefs within a relationship can be challenging, even among the most committed partners. Varied faiths, political views, or moral perspectives can present challenges that require thoughtful consideration.

Beliefs, seemingly a small topic on the surface, encompass many issues, making them critical in a relationship. It's essential to be mindful of how discussions about your partner's beliefs unfold. If you inadvertently offend your partner by crossing a line, their response signals the need for careful handling.

Political discussions, especially in today's digital age, can quickly spiral out of control. While expressing opinions on social media is one thing, bringing political tensions into your home can become a significant problem.

Being in a relationship with differing religious views may lead to stress if not managed properly. Active participation in each other's lives, especially in matters of tradition, is crucial for building a strong union. Opting out of fundamental practices can create alienation and a division between partners.

Respecting your partner's beliefs is paramount for a lasting relationship. The key to enduring relationships lies in continual growth, development, and mutual respect for individual goals and beliefs. Take the time to celebrate each other and find joy in your differences, transforming them into opportunities for discovery.

Beliefs Tool: Mutual Respect

Embracing differences in beliefs within a relationship is essential, even if your partner holds strong views different from your own, particularly regarding religion, politics, children, or societal functioning. Alignment on these aspects can ease the pressure, but when differences arise, employing the Mutual Respect tool becomes crucial. Allow your partner the space to have a distinct viewpoint without harboring hate or hostility. Effective communication and the wise principle of agreeing to disagree are key.

In a rapidly changing world where political and health discussions dominate conversations, it's common for differences to be met with resistance, especially on social media. If your partner's beliefs come under attack, you must defend and protect them.

Drawing from the skills learned, such as compromise and stopping judgment, it's crucial to refrain from asserting your viewpoint simply to make a point. Remember that everyone has a right to their own opinion. Approach conversations about differing beliefs with genuine curiosity and respect for your partner.

Encourage open and honest expression of thoughts and feelings without judgment, ridicule, or rejection based on differing beliefs. Avoid entering conversations intending to change your partner's thoughts, which often leads to failure.

Effective communication, characterized by active listening, is vital in overcoming differences. Actively listen without distractions or judgment, responding without letting emotions escalate. Talk with the intention to understand, not to win. Validate your partner's perspective, even if you don't agree, and create space for mutual growth and respect.

Disrespect

When you respect your partner, others will respect you

Respect is the cornerstone of a solid and meaningful relationship. It involves accepting your partner for who they are, even in moments of disagreement. Cultivating care in your relationships builds trust, a sense of security, and overall well-being, essential elements for achieving equality within a partnership.

Here, we delve deeper into factors that significantly impact your relationship and guide you in addressing them as a united and supportive team. To establish a true partnership, both individuals must feel a sense of equality. When disrespect creeps in, it undermines this balance, posing a threat to the very foundation of your connection. Listening attentively when your partner speaks and engaging in open, honest communication are fundamental ways to demonstrate respect. Any dishonesty, even in seemingly trivial matters, reflects a lack of respect.

Valuing your partner's time is another crucial aspect of respect. Prioritizing them in your daily and future plans conveys thoughtfulness and consideration. On the contrary, resorting to silent treatment or manipulative tactics when unhappy indicates a complete absence of respect.

While recognizing that nobody is perfect, intentionally hurting your partner's feelings during heated arguments is a disrespectful behavior that should be avoided. In a healthy partnership, both individuals willingly support each other by attending family functions as a united team, even if these activities may not always be the most enjoyable. Establishing and honoring each other's intimate or daily boundaries is vital for a thriving relationship. Refraining from disregarding or repetitively crossing these boundaries signifies a lack of respect.

Acknowledging the significance of respect in your partnership lays the foundation for a more fulfilling and harmonious connection. It's through mutual respect that a relationship thrives and stands firm against the challenges that may arise.

Disrespect Tool: Lead By Example

Using the "Lead by Example" tool to uphold respectful communication habits is essential. This involves carefully choosing and consciously using your words. Speak words of acknowledgment, appreciation, and gratitude for your partner's actions and who they are as individuals. Refrain from making comparisons to others if highlighting your partner's strengths. Replace sarcasm with gentle and kind language, avoiding dismissive gestures or contemptuous behavior. When facing complaints, communicate directly with your partner rather than venting to others. Ensure that your communication is accessible from impatience and irritability.

Respecting your partner's trust and confidentiality is paramount. Safeguard their intimate details and personal information, refraining from violating their privacy by sharing private matters with others.
In moments of conflict or disagreement, engage in constructive dialogue. Spar respectfully with your partner to work through differences, ultimately finding common ground and resolving issues. When expressing a complaint, be cautious not to criticize your partner's character but to address specific concerns.

Avoid the urge to assert control over your partner or establish boundaries that restrict their decision-making autonomy. Genuine mutual respect involves valuing their perspective and recognizing their ability to make choices. If you find yourself attempting to control or limit your partner, it signals a lack of mutual respect. Remember that your partner may not confront you directly, but their feelings will undoubtedly impact the relationship. Remember the saying, 'If you don't have something nice to say, don't say anything at all'—but take it a step further. Silence can also hurt. Unspoken frustrations, passive aggression, or emotional withdrawal can slowly erode connection and trust. Open, respectful communication is key to maintaining emotional safety and fostering a deeper understanding between partners.

Selfishness

Selfishness is not letting your partner live as they wish to live, it is asking your partner to live as you wish them to live

Being selfish in a romantic relationship can harm the dynamics between you and your partner and foster resentment and animosity. While maintaining individuality and pursuing personal goals is essential, considering and respecting your partner's needs is equally crucial. Here are the additional factors that can impact your partnership, which we'll address later in the book:

Selfishness is rooted in a self-centered mindset, prioritizing "I" over "we," the foundation of a healthy relationship. Relationships thrive on togetherness, both physically and emotionally. Building a sense of togetherness becomes challenging when a partner consistently disregards feelings. Selfish individuals hinder relationship growth by prioritizing their interests over shared goals, leading to hurt, disappointment, and resentment.

Being selfish involves constantly wanting things to go your way and exerting control over every aspect of your life, including your partner's. It neglects your partner's goals and thoughts, focusing solely on what you perceive as best. Letting go of excessive control is essential.

Signs of a selfish partner include having an "it's my way or the highway" attitude, dismissing your partner's opinions, avoiding accountability, expecting your partner to change while refusing to change yourself, consistently prioritizing your needs over your partner's, seeking control at all times, rarely celebrating your partner's happiness, taking your partner for granted, constantly taking without giving back, lacking empathy towards your partner, and acting impulsively without flexibility.

Selfishness Tool: WE

No matter how deeply you love someone, it's crucial to recognize that love alone may not be sufficient. There might be instances where, consciously or unconsciously, you neglect to consider your partner's feelings—expecting them to cook for you or zoning out when they share their day.

Selfishness, always wanting things your way and controlling every aspect of your life and your partner's, raises questions about the 'WE' in your partnership and equality. Reflect on whether this lack of compromise and communication is fair to your partner.

Activate the 'WE' tool by introspecting. Ask yourself if you exhibit selfish behavior—prioritizing your wants over needs, holding unspoken expectations, or resenting your partner when things don't align with yours.

If so, it's time to rectify the situation. Embrace open communication instead of resorting to silent treatment under challenging conversations. Avoid insisting your perspective is the only correct one. Recognize the importance of mutual support, actively listen when your partner vents, and refrain from routinely accusing them of selfishness.

Criticizing their friends and family excessively and ignoring their needs signal self-centeredness.

Threatening to end the relationship when things don't go your way reflects a lack of consideration for the 'WE' in your partnership.

Keep going when your partner addresses a significant problem. Acknowledge differing opinions and agree to disagree if needed. Share your strong opinions openly, but understand they have the right to oppose or not support demands they disagree with.

Don't punish them for not meeting your needs.
You can only need some things precisely when and how you want it.

Trivial matters like dinner choices, vacation destinations, or car types can become significant acts of selfishness. Let your partner have a voice, foster mutual respect, and avoid nurturing unspoken expectations.

Responsibilities

If you think your partner's place is in the kitchen, also remember that's where the knives are kept.

If you think your partner's place is in the kitchen, also remember that's where the knives are kept. A partnership implies working together, where stability, loyalty, and collaboration are essential. However, the seemingly simple concept of sharing responsibilities can become a source of fights, divorces, unhappiness, and resentment.

Issues often arise when one partner desires more active involvement from the other in the relationship. Even if one partner justifies being busy with work, providing financial support alone isn't enough. The key is to be present in the relationship both mentally and emotionally.

Calling outside help may get the job done, but it rarely replaces genuine teamwork. If one partner isn't contributing their fair share—whether it's housework, emotional support, parenting, planning, or simply showing up—it places an unfair burden on the other. That imbalance breeds resentment and begins to quietly erode the foundation of the relationship.

Entitlement has no place in a healthy partnership. Thinking you're "doing your part" might not align with your partner's experience. What you call balanced, they might experience as lopsided. The remedy? Communication, empathy, and a willingness to shift.

Ask your partner directly how they feel about the distribution of responsibilities. Don't wait for resentment to manifest as silence, sarcasm, or emotional withdrawal. Get ahead of the storm by listening. If you discover you've been lacking, the most powerful words might be, "You're right, I'm wrong."

Then act accordingly. Real partnership is built on humility, effort, and shared accountability. It's not about keeping score—it's about showing up. Consistently. Generously. Willingly.

And remember: being a responsible partner isn't a favor—it's a fundamental.

132

Responsibilitie Tool: Just Shut Up and Do It

It takes work to get on the same page with your partner and figure out what you each need. The goal is to tackle them together as partners, not commando solo. Be the wise and intelligent partner who kicks in and applies the "Just Shut Up and Do It" tool.

The first part of Just Shut Up and Do It is a compromise, and the second is organizing. This is the key to tackling all the tasks at hand. Remember, chores aren't just about cleaning. Paying bills, sitting on hold with the cable company, planning meals, and buying birthday gifts for family members are also essential.

Make lists of tasks in the following weeks and a calendar to show who is responsible for what tasks. Make a schedule and set deadlines. Set a reminder from a to-do list app or post the list of everyone, If one partner gets buried, the other should know to Just Shut Up and Do It. It's a partnership,and it takes a team to win a game.

Split the activities evenly. Start by assigning activities based on areas you're good at. The secret to avoiding the same old arguments is to complete your list of activities. If a partner isn't pulling their weight, call them out.

You must be careful in sharing activities based on who is better at a task, especially when it's an unbalanced list. If this is the case, your partner needs to learn new skills. Teach them how to chop an onion, or load a dishwasher. But do not criticize them or redo things because you don't like how it was done. This will only get your partner to check out and never do it again.

Then, get organized and apply those time management skills you've learned. For example, you must put in one hour of hard labor every two hours you play. The goal is to complete the honey-do list and, when done, ask for more. Think of it as "It's so much better to drive my car knowing the brakes actually work. "OMG, I can invite friends over now since they can no longer fall through that hole in the porch floor."

Voice

If your partner needs a voice.
Then Let Them Be Heard

In In a healthy partnership, both individuals should feel safe to speak, to be heard, and to matter. Thoughts, opinions, emotions, and concerns deserve space—not just to be aired, but to be acknowledged and respected. When one partner's voice is silenced, ignored, or consistently overshadowed, cracks begin to form beneath the surface.

Here are some factors that can quietly damage the foundation of your relationship:

Discarding personal values or beliefs without recognition or respect.
Every individual brings their own set of values into a relationship. These shouldn't be silenced—they should be celebrated. Authenticity fuels connection. Affirm your identity and encourage your partner to do the same. Falling into dominant and passive roles.

When one partner always leads and the other always follows, resentment brews. True partnership means balance—both voices, both perspectives, equally honored. Decisions should be made together, not dictated.

Letting fear, fatigue, or emotions silence expression.

Sometimes it's easier to stay quiet. But silence can be misinterpreted as indifference. Reclaim your voice, even when it shakes. Say what you feel. Say what you need. Your words matter.

Sacrificing personal happiness for the sake of keeping the peace.
Compromise should never mean erasure. Stay connected to the things that light you up—your hobbies, passions, friendships, and goals. A thriving relationship is built by two whole individuals, not one person disappearing for the other.

Voice Tool: Engaged Listening

Are You Silencing Your Partner's Voice? Engage the "Engaged Listening" Tool.

Respect and Acknowledgment: Do you tend to overshadow your partner's voice with your opinions, failing to acknowledge and respect their thoughts?

Dreams and Support: Do you dismiss your partner's dreams and ideals or encourage and support them, fostering a positive environment?

Independence vs. Support: Do you insult and lack support, leaving your partner to handle matters independently, or are you there to assist?

Listening Time: When your partner has exciting news, do you make time to listen or brush it off due to busyness or feeling overwhelmed?

Communication Style: Are you prone to interrupt or raise your voice during discussions, hindering your partner from expressing recurring problems?

Anger Management: Have you let anger escalate to losing control or becoming physically aggressive, silencing your partner's voice?

If any of these resonate, it's time to use the "Engaged Listening" tool. Establish a genuine partnership based on love, respect, and integrity.

In Decision-Making: Consider your partner's opinions, especially in planning a trip or major financial decisions. Empower them to make choices.

Balanced Conversations: Ensure your partner's opinions are heard and acknowledged. Adjust your tone to avoid overpowering and Never resort to violence.

Supportive Communication: Be positive and loving during discussions, especially when seeking advice. Show support when interacting with others.

The solution is treating your partner equally, valuing their voice, and fostering a partnership where both voices matter. Embrace engaged listening for a relationship built on mutual respect and empowerment.

EQUALITY PILLAR

Resenyment

Commitment

Co-dependency

keep scoring

Baggage Issues
Tools to Repair
The Equality Pillar

Unresolved problems that one or both partners
bring into the relationship.

Co-dependency

Unraveling Codependency in Your Partnership

Codependency, while rooted in good intentions, poses challenges to the well-being of both partners. Recognizing signs of codependency is crucial, as it leads to imbalances where personal needs and self-worth take a backseat.

Root Causes of Codependency: Compensating for Past Deficiencies: Codependency often arises from a deep desire to pay for past deficiencies, attempting to make up for what was lacking or never received.

"Mama's Boy Syndrome": In some cases, unspoken reverence for a parent, often mothers, may lead to difficulty expressing negative emotions or setting boundaries with them while freely expressing anger towards the partner.

Desire for Control: Codependency may manifest as a desire for control extending to partners and children. This can impede healthy child development and perpetuate codependent patterns across generations.

Impact on Relationships: Imbalance and Sidelining Needs: Overly caretaking behaviors can create an imbalance where one partner's needs are prioritized, sidelining the importance of the other's needs and self-worth.

Parental Role and Impact on Children: Codependency can affect children by shaping their identities, values, and emotional dependency. Routines may overshadow genuine family time and connection.

Breaking the Cycle of Codependency: Means recognizing and addressing codependency involves acknowledging and healing past wounds, fostering self-awareness, and understanding the roots of these behaviors.

Establishing human boundaries is crucial. It allows both partners to maintain individual identities and needs within the relationship.

By breaking the cycle of codependency, couples can cultivate relationships founded on mutual respect, support, and the freedom to express authentic selves. Addressing codependency warmly and caringly is a transformative step toward healthier partnerships.

Co-dependency Tool: Bad Programing

If codependency lingers in your relationship, approaching the issue with understanding and compassion is crucial. Recognize that codependency often originates from past traumas or experiences of abandonment, significantly impacting self-esteem and potentially leading to depression. Addressing the core of these issues is essential for dismantling codependency and facilitating your partner's healing.

Caution and Patience: Approach discussions about sensitive topics with caution and patience. Understand that opening up about painful wounds might initially cause your partner to withdraw or shut down. Be a strong and patient partner willing to gather puzzle pieces of information individually.

Encouraging Open Dialogue: Significant progress is achieved when your partner can openly discuss the heart of the problem. They aim to share their secrets, enabling them to put the past behind them and embark on a healing journey. Seek professional help if these discussions becomes challenging.

Moving Forward: Frame conversations around leaving the past behind and embracing the present. Avoid blaming external factors and focus on taking control of your own actions. Consciously reject negative thoughts and redirect your focus to a happier place.

Eliminating Toxic Influences: Eliminate toxic influences from your life that lack respect. Surround yourself intentionally with positive and supportive people who celebrate your accomplishments and achievements.

Discovering a New Identity: Through personal growth, you may find a new version of yourself—an accurate and independent self not defined by others opinion. Stop blaming others for past actions.

Prioritizing Positive Relationships: Surround yourself with individuals who radiate positivity and happiness. Consult with your partner if unsure about changes needed for codependent friends affecting your partnership. and evolve together. Life can be extraordinary when those closest to you evolve alongside you. Allow others a chance to make a positive difference in your life, remembering to give them time to get to know the real you.

Commitment

Commitment Challenges in Relationships

Commitment issues can pose significant challenges in forming and maintaining successful partnerships and transcending generational boundaries. When one partner struggles with total commitment, it gives profoundly impact the relationship. These challenges stem from personal experiences, fears, and insecurities, shaping the partnership dynamics.

Past Traumas: Experiences like the departure of a parent or a loved one can instill feelings of neglect and unworthiness, fostering a constant fear of losing the current partner. This fear may manifest as jealousy and trust issues, creating a barrier to wholeheartedly investing in the relationship.

Some individuals with a dismissive personality type desire independence even within close relationships. Fear of getting hurt or betrayed leads them to maintain emotional distance, hindering full engagement in the partnership.

Constant worry about not being worthy of love can impede their ability to fully commit, questioning their capacity to meet their partner's expectations.

Lack of commitment can lead to instability during conflicts, with the immediate impulse being to leave rather than work towards resolution.

Commitment issues may result in emotional and physical distance, affecting intimacy and connection within the partnership.

Grass-Is-Greener Mentality: A perpetual dissatisfaction with the relationship may lead to seeking validation outside, jeopardizing the partnership.

A lack of commitment can impede personal growth, with the individual feeling constrained by their partner's presence.

Partners must approach commitment issues with empathy and patience, recognizing the problems that arise when commitment is lacking.

By working together, partners can rebuild trust, foster a deeper connection, and cultivate a strong foundation of commitment in their partnership.

Commitment Tool: Identity

Rekindling Commitment: The "IDENTITY" Tool

If you question your commitment to the partnership, it's time to take proactive steps to reignite the flame of love and dedication. The "IDENTITY" tool is designed to demonstrate unwavering commitment in your relationship.

Share your commitment openly with your partner and consider granting access to personal information as a symbol of trust.

Consciously eliminate activities that indicate a lack of dedication. Come home at reasonable hours, limit time with friends and hobbies, and actively contribute to household responsibilities.

Fulfill Commitments: Actively fulfill commitments, including long-overdue tasks, to demonstrate your dedication.

Beyond Chemistry and Compatibility: Genuine relationships go beyond chemistry and compatibility; they are founded on commitment. Commitment involves continual give and take, extending beyond persevering through tough times. In genuine commitment, your partner becomes your tireless advocate, defending you even when undeserved.

A committed partnership involves sharing deep secrets, vulnerabilities, fears, and strengths, strengthening the bond of trust and connection. Committed partners can handle difficult conversations and navigate sensitive topics.

Committed partners spend most of their time together, feeling inseparable and deeply connected. Take a moment to reflect on these questions: Are you truly committed to your partner? Do you genuinely need them in your life? Embracing commitment means recognizing your partner's profound impact on your well-being, happiness, and growth. It involves acknowledging their irreplaceable role in your life and actively prioritizing and nurturing the partnership.

By affirming your commitment and recognizing the significance of your partner's presence, you lay the groundwork for a relationship that flourishes with love, trust, and mutual respect. Embrace the journey of unwavering commitment, knowing that the rewards of a deeply fulfilling partnership.

Keeping Score

The Pitfalls of Keeping Score in a Partnership

When one or both partners engage in the harmful habit of keeping score in a relationship, it introduces a toxic dynamic that can erode the foundation of trust and mutual understanding. The act of tallying perceived slights, favors, or contributions can lead to many problems, negatively impacting the overall health of the partnership.

Keeping score often breeds resentment and animosity as partners fixate on perceived give-and-take imbalances. Constantly monitoring and comparing contributions can erode trust, creating an atmosphere of suspicion and insecurity. The focus on scorekeeping can lead to a decreased emotional connection, as partners prioritize perceived debts over genuine emotional support.

Partners may refrain from open communication about their needs and expectations, fearing it will be used against them in the scorekeeping game. It can spark power struggles, turning simple disagreements into battles where each partner seeks to prove their point and gain the upper hand.

The fixation on scores tends to overshadow the meaningful acts of love and kindness, diminishing the overall positive atmosphere in the relationship. Intimacy suffers when partners are preoccupied with scorekeeping, as it diverts focus from shared moments and connection.

Partners adopt a tit-for-tat mentality, expecting equal reciprocation for every action or favor. There is a tendency to catalog and remember perceived grievances, creating a mental tally of who owes what. Partners maintain a mental scorecard, tracking each other's contributions and shortcomings.

Escalation of Conflict: Scorekeeping can escalate conflicts, turning minor disagreements into full-blown arguments fueled by past grievances.Fear of not receiving equal returns can stifle partners' willingness to be generous, leading to a transactional rather than a giving relationship. Partners may emotionally withdraw, fearing that vulnerability will be used against them.

142

Keeping Score Tool: Teamwork

Breaking Free from Scorekeeping: The Power of Teamwork

To dismantle the destructive habit of scorekeeping in your partnership, the key lies in embracing the "TEAMWORK" tool. This approach emphasizes collaboration, open communication, and a shared commitment to building a relationship founded on mutual support.

Approach the situation with honesty and vulnerability, acknowledging that scorekeeping hinders relationship growth. Demonstrate self-awareness and maturity by recognizing instances where you may have fallen into the trap of scorekeeping. When your partner highlights oversights or shortcomings, resist the urge to become defensive or counterattack.

Take ownership of your actions, apologize sincerely, and actively work towards minimizing imbalances. Actively divide tasks, considering household chores, childcare, financial responsibilities, and other significant activities. Treat your relationship as a team, collaborating to find an equitable distribution of responsibilities based on availability, strengths, and preferences.

Foster open communication about needs and concerns related to task distribution. Express how certain behaviors or imbalances impact you and the relationship, creating an environment of empathy and understanding. Avoid blaming or accusing your partner of laziness or selfishness; instead, focus on the impact of their actions. Create a positive space where your partner is more likely to respond positively and work collaboratively towards solutions.

Understand that achieving balance doesn't mean demanding equal participation in every task. Prioritize effective communication to find a division of labor that respects each other's preferences and contributions.

By actively implementing the TEAMWORK tool, partners can overcome the trap of scorekeeping and shift the focus toward mutual support and shared goals. Rather than measuring who does more, the emphasis becomes collaboration, appreciation, and maintaining a healthy rhythm that works for both partners.

Resentment

Navigating Resentment: Overcoming Challenges in Your Partnership

Resentment is like a slow-burning fuse. Left unchecked, it can silently smolder beneath the surface of a relationship, eventually exploding in ways that damage trust, intimacy, and connection. It's not just about anger—it's about unspoken disappointment, unresolved hurt, and emotional fatigue.

Understanding the roots of resentment is essential for healing and rebuilding. Here's where it often begins: Resentment within a partnership can pose significant challenges, straining the connection between partners and giving rise to feelings of anger, disappointment, and hurt. Understanding the factors that contribute to resentment is crucial for healing and restoring the relationship.

Common Triggers for Resentment: Selfish behaviors, Excessive focus on work, Irresponsible spending habits, Prioritizing one side of the family over the other, Lack of presence and engagement at home or with the children, Unreasonable expectations on the partner, Neglecting to acknowledge, important occasions or holidays and Identifying Resentment:

Continuous recycling of feelings of anger without seeking resolution like Dwelling on past mistakes or decisions or Avoidance of confrontation or deflection when issues arise will bring resentment:

Resentment is not always about what's done to us—but also about what we allow to fester without addressing. The key is open, honest, and empathetic communication. Both partners need to create a space where truth can be spoken without fear. If you're the one holding resentment, speak your truth with clarity—not accusation. If you're on the receiving end, listen with humility—not defensiveness. Either way, resolution only comes through mutual accountability and a shared desire to restore balance.

Because love can't breathe where resentment lives. But when both partners commit to clearing the air, something better can emerge—real connection, real trust, and real partnership.

Resentment Tool: Forgive

A crucial aspect of using the "Forgive" tool is to offer a genuine apology without following it with justifications, explanations, or defenses. A sincere apology acknowledges your actions without attempting to justify them.

If tension permeates the room, it's time to address the root of the problem. Start by exploring the origins of your resentment and try to understand your partner's perspective. Acknowledging your role in triggering your partner's behavior and taking ownership of your actions is crucial. The "Forgive" tool can be invaluable in releasing the weight of resentment.

Sit down with your partner and establish agreements on how you will treat each other and what is acceptable and unacceptable. These commitments will prevent future resentment-inducing and will foster mutual respect.

If you're feeling resentful, likely, your partner is already aware of it. Instead of allowing wounds to fester, be honest and transparent about your emotions and invite your partner to collaborate on finding solutions. Focus on what you can control, letting go of past hurts, and making better choices and take responsibility for your part in conflicts or disputes.

Emotional detachment and a decline in sexual intimacy rarely occur overnight. Resentment often hides beneath the surface. Approach your partner with vulnerability and care, inquiring if you've done anything that has bothered them or caused hurt. While it may be challenging to hear their answer, remain receptive and avoid becoming defensive, resolving resentment requires both partners to work together.

By addressing resentment head-on, embracing vulnerability, and practicing open communication, you can begin the journey of healing and rebuilding trust in your partnership. Remember that it takes time and effort, but the rewards are a deeper connection and a more fulfilling relationship. Allow both partners to express grievances without judgment or defensiveness.

A conscious decision to move forward and rebuild trust. Commitment to overcoming past grievances. By addressing and resolving resentment, partners can lay the groundwork for a relationship characterized by mutual understanding, respect, and Overcoming resentment requires patience, empathy, and a genuine desire to heal and strengthen the bond.

146

Chapter 9:
Daily Tools for Relationship Security

Emotional Support

The Scars you can't see are the hardest to heal

Lack of emotional support for men can manifest in various ways, such as feeling emotionally distant, hesitating to discuss feelings, leading separate lives, struggling to listen to your partner's concerns, or experiencing a decline in physical intimacy. It might be a sign that emotional support is lacking if you find yourself emotionally distant or hesitant to open up about your feelings.

Leading Separate Lives:
Partners leading separate lives without actively participating in each other's experiences can lead to emotional detachment. Being present and engaged in each other's lives is crucial for providing and receiving emotional support.

Facing challenges in actively listening to your partner's problems can impede emotional support. Demonstrating genuine interest and empathy is vital for effective communication and support, fostering a deeper connection.

A noticeable decrease in physical intimacy may stem from emotional disconnection. Emotional support is instrumental in maintaining both emotional and physical bonds between partners.

While providing emotional support is crucial, men must be mindful of preventing emotional exhaustion. Striking a balance between supporting their partner and practicing self-care is essential for maintaining a healthy relationship.

Recognize and celebrate both significant and small achievements of your partner. Share their joy and express enthusiasm when they share good news or achieve milestones.

Emotional Support Tool: Validation

In the foundation of solid partnerships lies the crucial element of emotional support, and a highly effective tool for achieving this is "Validation."

Emotional support encompasses providing love, reassurance, acceptance, and encouragement in a relationship, free from bias or judgment and critical during times of stress or sadness, serving as a means to be your partner's unwavering support and a steadfast foundation when they need it most.

You can contribute to uplifting and cultivating your partnership. The critical question to ask yourself is: Are you that person? Employ the tool of validation using expressions like "I'M PROUD of YOU," "I LOVE YOU," and "I NEED YOU" to empower and emotionally fortify your partner.

When your partner faces difficult times, give your full support. Refrain from holding back or downplaying their struggles. Having the person you love beside you during challenging moments is an invaluable gift.

Do you respect your partner's emotions when they express them? Are you an attentive listener, emotionally present to provide support? Do you communicate disagreements with love and compassion? Do you avoid judging or dismissing your partner's ideas without thoughtful consideration? Are you open with your partner and express admiration in front of others? Do you communicate to others how much your partner means to you?

Never underestimate the significance of acknowledging your loved one's presence. Few things are more hurtful than feeling like you don't matter, especially in anger. Knowing you are heard can be incredibly nurturing and healing. Speak with love and care, reinforcing emotional connection.

There are numerous ways to express love; uttering the three powerful words, "I love you," just reassures your partner. However, avoid automated or routine expressions so that when you say "I love you," it carries genuine weight.

If you are deeply in love, express it through these words. If you are madly in love, let it be known. If you genuinely cherish your partner, use these words to convey your feelings. Enhance the expression of love by adding gestures like a kiss, holding hands, or sharing a meaningful gaze. Remember, actions and words of validation and love complement each other harmoniously.

Feeling Loved

*All great things are simple and can be
contained in a single word: hope.*

The problem with feeling loved in a partnership often arises when one fails to take ownership and bring security into the relationship. This responsibility rests solely on the individual, who has the power to make a positive impact by letting their actions lead. Owning the partnership involves prioritizing one's partner as the most critical person in their life, even above family and children. It means not allowing external influences to dictate the partnership dynamics and ensuring the partner's voice is heard.

Critical mistakes, such as criticism, degradation, arguments, attacks, or negative statements, as outlined in Chapter 2, can be highly detrimental to any relationship. If these mistakes persist, the relationship may be on a rapid path towards feeling loveless.

Emotional shutdowns or avoidance of significant issues create distance within the partnership, negatively impacting the love shared between partners. Constant anger or yelling erodes the ability to express and receive love, leading to a dynamic where partners become akin to bad roommates.

If one partner lacks love, the other partner likely experiences the same. Mutual loss of respect and emotions like anger and resentment can push both individuals to question the purpose of remaining in such a miserable partnership.

The absence of love poses a significant threat to a partnership. To initiate a positive change, it is crucial to take ownership of the situation and acknowledge, "You're right, I'm wrong." This admission opens the door to addressing the issues, rebuilding respect, and fostering a more loving and fulfilling partnership.

A lack of love can hurt a partnership. If this has happened and you want to turn it around, then own it and say, "You're right, I'm wrong."

Feeling Loved Tool: Hope

The solution to rebuilding a sense of love in the partnership involves using the Hope tool.

When your partner entered a committed relationship with you, there was an inherent hope that the commitment would last forever. The crucial question is whether your partner still feels you are committed to being there for them in the long run or if your actions convey a desire to abandon ship.

The Hope Tool emphasizes the importance of making your partner the top priority to reignite love in the relationship. This involves a return to basics and a commitment to prioritizing your partner's needs. While the solution is simple, it requires sacrifice, letting go of past grievances, and recognizing that the relationship is not solely about individual needs.

To implement the Hope Tool, initiate a conversation with your partner and openly discuss the issues that bother them. Express your genuine desire for them to love, respect, and trust you again, and communicate your readiness to make positive changes.

Utilize the Three-Day Rule learned in Chapter 4 to effectively address concerns. Compile a list of issues, take three days to process them without judgment, and resist the initial defensive response. After calming down, review the list, identify reasonable changes, and, for more complex issues, engage in a dialogue with your partner to find compromises. This approach demonstrates to your partner that they are a priority in your life.

Commitment is crucial in this process. Stay positive through the ups and downs, discard negative thoughts, and remember that actions speak louder than words. As the rock in the relationship, your partner relies on you, and by making them a priority, you turn hope into a reality. Making your partner a priority is not complicated; it requires commitment.

Finances

It's senseless to fight about money,
because after you said all those mean things to each other,
the amount of money in the bank is still the same

The problem with finances in a partnership can manifest in various ways, leading to conflicts, arguments, and potential deceitful behavior. Financial disagreements can jeopardize the sense of security within the relationship, making it crucial to address these issues collaboratively. Several factors contribute to economic challenges in a partnership:

Disagreements over money can lead to conflicts and breaches of trust. Differing financial perspectives without clear resolutions may contribute to ongoing disputes.

One partner must consult the other to make significant financial decisions. It may stem from believing the partner wouldn't understand or agree. Encouraging open communication and involving both partners in financial matters is essential.

Financial Literacy Disparities: Differences in financial knowledge or skills between partners can impact money management strategies. Offering guidance or suggesting classes to improve financial literacy can be beneficial, ensuring both partners are involved in budgeting and decision-making.

Unequal distribution of responsibility for monthly bills can lead to burdens and extra work. Allocating personal spending money and collaboratively establishing a budget can address these concerns and promote shared financial responsibilities.

Open communication is crucial when considering significant purchases. Financial matters may sometimes cross boundaries within a partnership. In such cases, humility and a willingness to compromise become vital.

Approaching financial challenges as a team with open communication, respect, and a shared commitment to economic well-being allows partners to navigate the complexities of finances. By doing so, they can build a stronger, more secure partnership.

Finances Tool: Cooperative Behavior

The problem in the financial aspect of a partnership often arises due to differing money mindsets and approaches to finances between individuals. One person may be inclined towards saving, while the other may adopt a more carefree attitude towards spending. To ensure a sense of security in the partnership, accurate information about finances must be provided to the partner.

Cooperative behavior tool is crucial in addressing financial challenges. Compromise becomes essential in determining spending patterns, and effective communication is vital before making significant financial decisions. This collaborative approach sets the foundation for managing finances harmoniously within the partnership.

Establishing a financial plan as a couple early on and either sticking to it or making necessary adjustments exemplifies actual cooperative behavior. Different strategies can be employed, such as maintaining separate bank accounts alongside a joint account for shared expenses. This allows for independence while actively participating in household financial management. Partners may opt for a single joint account for all income and expenses, fostering unity and transparency.

The key is to find a financial arrangement that best suits the partnership, considering factors like individual spending habits and preferences. Open communication and addressing concerns are crucial in maintaining a healthy and balanced approach to finances within the partnership. Cooperative behavior, characterized by regular communication, understanding, and mutual decision-making, contributes to financial harmony and strengthens the bond between partners.

Jealousy

The real power of love
is the size of your partner's smile when they sit next to you

When unchecked, jealousy can pose a significant challenge to a partnership. This book recognizes the impact of jealousy on the security pillar of a relationship and provides guidance on managing and overcoming this emotion as a team.

Distinguishing between healthy and unhealthy jealousy is essential. While occasional jealousy can be a natural and beneficial aspect of a relationship, it becomes problematic when it intensifies, becomes irrational, and consumes one's thoughts and actions.

Jealousy typically arises in response to perceived threats, real or imagined, to a valued relationship. While a certain level of jealousy is average, excessive jealousy can lead to dangerous behaviors, such as stalking, digital dating violence, and even physical abuse.

Addressing jealousy requires self-awareness and effort. If overwhelmed by jealousy, having an open and honest conversation with your partner about your emotions and exploring the underlying reasons can be beneficial. Similarly, if your partner displays unreasonable jealousy, addressing this toxic emotion is crucial to prevent harm to the partnership. Jealousy often stems from personal insecurities, such as self-doubt or comparing oneself to others.

Dealing with jealousy involves recognizing triggers, managing suspicion, and understanding that irrational jealousy is not a sign of love but a distortion. If jealousy leads to losing control and crossing boundaries, acknowledging this and making amends is crucial. The book emphasizes the importance of saying, "You're right, I'm wrong," to foster understanding and growth within the partnership.

Jealousy Tool: It's Just Wrong

Jealousy is an inevitable emotion in relationships, often from a fear of losing someone you care about. While occasional jealousy is natural, it becomes problematic when not handled effectively. Whether triggered by your partner's connections or your own tendencies, understanding the root causes is crucial. Communicating openly with your partner about these feelings and being honest can prevent escalation. Jealousy, when moderate, can intensify emotions, but it's essential to avoid letting imagination overpower reality. The "IT'S JUST WRONG" tool is introduced to address these issues.

Jealousy can manifest in various forms, and abnormal jealousy often stems from immaturity, insecurity, or an unhealthy need for control. Acknowledging the issue is the first step, exploring whether it's rooted in trust issues, past experiences, or feelings of inadequacy. Avoiding behaviors that provoke jealousy, such as flirting or seeking excessive attention from others, is crucial. The tool emphasizes recognizing that such actions are just wrong and detrimental to the partnership's security.

While a certain level of jealousy is average, when it leads to your partner feeling threatened, it becomes your responsibility to address their pain and make them feel secure again. Understanding the root causes of jealousy, spending quality time together, and building a solid emotional bond is vital. Reflect on why jealousy arises and challenge irrational thoughts that trigger your partner's jealousy.

Improving self-esteem is essential, as irrational jealousy often stems from a lack of self-worth. Vulnerability and emotional intimacy play crucial roles in a successful relationship. Each person needs to take risks for personal growth and connection. By implementing these strategies and utilizing the "IT'S JUST WRONG" tool, overcoming jealousy becomes possible, fostering a healthier and more secure partnership.

Manipulation

The art of pleasing your partner can also be the art of manipulating your partner

Controlling behavior in a person may stem from various reasons, with past trauma being a significant factor. Individuals who have experienced abuse or abandonment in childhood may exhibit controlling behavior to regain a sense of security and prevent further suffering. This need for control can impact the security pillar of a partnership. Another contributing factor is low self-confidence and self-esteem. Individuals who have faced consistent criticism or have a personality disorder affecting their self-confidence may resort to controlling behavior to feel superior and temporarily boost their confidence.

Manipulation often manifests as criticism, starting subtly and escalating over time. Guilt-tripping is another tactic where the controlling person makes their partner feel guilty for choices that don't align with their desires. This manipulative approach aims to enforce compliance. Isolation is a powerful strategy employed by controlling individuals, cutting off their partner from external influences and relationships to gain further control.

Recognizing manipulation and setting appropriate limits is crucial. The book emphasizes acknowledging and saying, "You're Right, I'm Wrong," to promote healthy communication and resolve conflicts. By addressing manipulation, partners can work towards fostering a partnership built on trust, respect, and open communication, thereby overcoming the detrimental impact of controlling behavior on the relationship's security.

Manipulation Tool: Stop

Manipulation should not be accepted as a standard in a healthy partnership, as it can erode trust, communication, and overall relationship satisfaction. Striving for open and honest communication, mutual respect, and equal decision-making is essential to overcome manipulation.

In addressing the manipulation problem, the "STOP" tool can bring awareness to manipulative behaviors and initiate positive changes. Recognizing the signs of manipulation and understanding its negative impact on the partnership is the first step toward addressing the issue.

Using the "STOP" tool is crucial if you engage in manipulative behaviors. Flip the LIGHT SWITCH and reflect on your actions and their effects on your partner. Instead of micromanagement, criticism, or limiting your partner's activities, strive for open dialogue, understanding, and compromise.

Dealing with a controlling partner requires remaining calm and collected. Avoid engaging in arguments or responding defensively. Seek to understand their perspective while respectfully asserting your thoughts and feelings. Constructive questions challenge unreasonable expectations or behavior.

Recognizing signs of manipulation, such as coercion, blame, criticism, or withholding, is crucial for addressing the issue. By being aware of these signs, you can assert boundaries, communicate your needs, and confront manipulative behaviors with assertiveness and respect.

It's important to note that controllers may deny their behavior or feel they are being controlled. Instead of attacking their character, focus on expressing how specific actions or situations impact the partnership. Encourage open dialogue and a willingness to address and overcome manipulative behaviors together.

Stress

*Sure, they can do it all by themselves,
but a real partner won't let them.*

Stress is a standard part of everyone's daily life, and as a partner, making a positive difference in how your significant other deals with and reduces stress is crucial. Stressful events can profoundly impact your partner's view of themselves and the world around them, influencing feelings about life, jobs, relationships, security, and the future. However, if you're emotionally disconnected, you may be unaware of these changes.

If you rely on your partner to handle all the household activities, you must recognize that you may unintentionally add stress to their life. Sometimes, your partner might feel they can't count on you for even the most minor tasks, leading them to handle everything themselves to avoid frustration.

Finding balance can be challenging when overwhelmed with finances, family, health, and work issues. This is especially true if one partner tends to carry most of the burden. Stress has the potential to create emotional distance, resulting in a loss of intimacy and the decline of romance in the relationship.

In a strong partnership where both partners actively manage stress, the ability to bounce back from challenges like loss, trauma, and tragedy is known as psychological resilience. However, these issues can become significant problems when a partnership is weak. Therefore, it's essential to actively engage in stress management together to foster a resilient and healthy relationship.

If your partner is always on pins and needles, then you haven't done your job. If this has happened and you want to turn it around, then own it and say, "You're right, I'm wrong."

Stress Tool: It's Your Job

Stress is a common aspect of daily life, and when one partner is overloaded, it can significantly impact the relationship. Financial concerns, household responsibilities, and a lack of quality time can contribute to stress, leading to emotional distance and potential damage to the partnership's security and resilience.

Solution with "It's Your Job" Tool:

The key to helping an overloaded partner is adopting the mindset that reducing their stress is your responsibility—make it your job. "It's Your Job" is a game-changer in stress management. When you notice signs of stress in your partner, approach them with kindness and compassion, asking how you can help or what you can do to make things better.

Utilize the skills learned in Chapter 4, such as compromise. Make dedicated time for your partner by temporarily canceling personal activities to focus solely on the relationship. If finances are a source of stress, work together to find solutions, even if it means making tough decisions like selling items or cutting unnecessary expenses.

Recognize the importance of intimacy and fun in the relationship. Make it your job to schedule activities that bring joy, such as movies, walks, picnics, games, and trips. Prioritize your relationship over other commitments, celebrate each other, and communicate openly and respectfully to avoid misunderstandings.

When making significant decisions, ensure your partner is involved and agrees with the choices. Being proficient in reducing stress means being honest and truthful with your partner, even when it is difficult. This honesty fosters trust, reduces secrets, and ultimately lessens stress in the relationship. Maintaining your partner's well-being is critical to building a resilient and healthy partnership.

Temper

*If you push your partner's buttons
too many times, they might just stop working.*

A bad temper can harm a partnership, causing various issues for both partners. If explosive behavior, yelling, threats, or name-calling are part of the norm, it creates an unhealthy environment. Uncontrolled anger can instill fear in your partner and family members, making them hesitant to express themselves or share differing opinions.

Acknowledge that a lousy temper negatively affects you and those around you. Understand that it can create an atmosphere of tension, fear, and walking on eggshells for your family.

Work on acquiring and implementing practical anger management skills. This may involve seeking professional help, attending anger management courses, or practicing techniques such as deep breathing, mindfulness, or cooling down before reacting.

Create an environment where open communication is encouraged. Let your partner and family know their opinions and feelings are valued, and they can express themselves without fear of triggering an explosive reaction.

Cultivate patience and understanding in dealing with everyday inconveniences or disagreements. Practice being more patient with yourself and those around you, recognizing that not every situation requires an angry response.

If you do lose your temper, own up to it. Acknowledge the mistake and take responsibility by saying, "You're right, I'm wrong." This demonstrates humility and a commitment to improving your behavior.

If the temper issues persist, consider seeking professional help. A therapist or counselor can provide guidance in understanding and managing your anger, as well as addressing any underlying issues contributing to the temper outbursts.

Temper Tool: Check Your Chatterbox

Regularly losing your temper and escalating minor issues into major problems is a sign of Chatterbox Syndrome. This internal dialogue refuses to let go, pushing you to lose control. To break this cycle and maintain a healthy relationship, it's crucial to Check Your Chatterbox.

Recognize situations or triggers that activate your Chatterbox, leading to anger. Understanding these triggers is the first step towards gaining control.

Practice counting to 10 and taking deep breaths to interrupt the automatic escalation initiated by the Chatterbox. Redirect your focus away from negative emotions, making the subconscious voice conscious for control.

Engage in positive activities or thoughts to distract yourself from negative feelings. Redirect your attention to more constructive aspects of your life to break the cycle of negativity.

If the Chatterbox persists and you feel overwhelmed, physically remove yourself. Take a break for a few minutes, exercise, walk, or meditate to release negative energy before returning to discuss the issue calmly.

Bring the subconscious voice to your conscious awareness. Analyze irrational thoughts and challenge them with rational thinking. This process enables you to control the Chatterbox and prevent it from escalating.

After calming down, engage in open communication with your partner. Express your concerns without losing control, focusing on being reasonable and constructive. Address the issues at hand with a mindset of finding mutually beneficial solutions.

In situations involving addictions or heated arguments, where making reasonable decisions is challenging, record your thoughts at the moment. This provides an outlet and allows you to revisit the discussion later.

Remember, fighting over every difference weakens the partnership. Focus on creating a positive environment, influencing your partner through cooperation, and allowing negative energy to cool down your Chatterbox.

Weight

Your partner can't change you.
But you can change because you love your partner.

Struggling with body image and weight issues is a personal challenge that can be further exacerbated when a partner engages in criticism or makes casual remarks about their appearance. This impacts the individual's self-esteem and creates a hostile atmosphere within the relationship.

The pervasive influence of societal beauty standards, often showcasing younger, skinny individuals, can contribute to feelings of inadequacy and frustration for those struggling with weight-related issues.

Criticizing or making casual one-liners about a partner's weight can lead to increased stress, anxiety, and a damaged sense of self-worth. It creates an unhealthy dynamic within the relationship, fostering insecurity and discomfort.

Weight-related comments can significantly impact a person's self-esteem, making it challenging to feel comfortable in their skin. This may lead to avoidance behaviors, such as not wanting to be seen undressed or in specific lighting.

For some individuals, dissatisfaction with their appearance can become obsessive and unhealthy. This may manifest in extreme dieting, excessive exercise, or other behaviors negatively impacting physical and mental well-being.

Constant criticism or negative remarks create a strained atmosphere in the relationship. It erodes the emotional connection between partners, making fostering trust, communication, and mutual understanding difficult.

Weight-related conversations can easily cross boundaries, leading to hurtful remarks and emotional distress. Such discussions may contribute to a breakdown in communication, hindering the ability to address the core issues in a supportive manner.

Weight Tool: It's Just a Number

In reality, weight is a problem for many, but driving your partner crazy about it is not the solution. Adopt the mindset of "It's Just a Number." Whether the number goes up or down, focus on supporting your partner on their terms and timeline with gentle encouragement.

Addressing weight-related challenges requires a shift in approach, focusing on support, understanding, and fostering a positive self-image. Embracing and supporting your partner's journey toward a healthier self-perception can lead to a more positive and nurturing relationship.

Encourage a positive self-image by expressing love and appreciation beyond physical appearance. Reinforce your partner's strengths, talents, and unique qualities, emphasizing that your love goes beyond external factors.

Refrain from making negative remarks or criticisms about your partner's weight. Choose supportive language that centers around overall well-being and emphasizes your commitment to their happiness.

Establish open communication about body image concerns, creating a safe space for your partner to share their feelings without judgment. Encourage discussions about struggles and aspirations, fostering emotional support.

Instead of pressuring your partner to conform to specific beauty standards, focus on adopting healthy habits together. Encourage activities that promote physical well-being, emphasizing overall health rather than appearance.

If weight-related conversations have crossed boundaries, apologize and acknowledge the impact of your words and eExpress genuine remorse.

Be there for your partner if they seek help. Walk their path, do their workout, and make changes together. Positive comments matter. Encourage your partner with positive affirmations and avoid negative remarks that can shut them down. Embrace the journey with the understanding that "It's Just a number and focus on the beauty within. Love your partner for who they are, not just what the scale says. Success is when your partner feels comfortable undressing in front of you with the lights on.

SECURITY PILLAR

Forgiveness

Abuse

Selfesteem

Financial Security

Baggage Issues
Tools to Repair
The Security Pillar

Unresolved problems that one or both partners
bring into the relationship.

Abuse

Addressing the abuse issue in a partnership is crucial for the mental and emotional well-being of all involved parties. Abuse can take various forms, including physical, psychological, or emotional harm.

Understanding the origins of abusive behavior, which may be linked to past experiences or childhood trauma, is essential. However, not all abusers come from abusive backgrounds, and in some cases, abusive dynamics may be normalized due to toxic family dynamics.

For individuals who have experienced sexual trauma or physical abuse, past trauma can resurface unexpectedly, leading to complex emotions and potential retraumatization. This can affect sexual intimacy and create challenges in the relationship. Similarly, partners who have been betrayed in past relationships may struggle with trust and boundary issues, impacting the establishment of safety within the current relationship.

Both partners must recognize the presence of abuse and its impact. Open and honest communication is critical but must be approached with empathy and understanding. Seeking professional help, such as therapy or counseling, provides a safe space to explore the underlying causes of abuse, heal from past traumas, and develop healthier patterns of interaction.

Addressing abuse requires a commitment from both partners to create a safe and supportive environment. Prioritizing the well-being of each individual is essential, working towards building a relationship based on trust, respect, and non-violence. It is a collective effort to break the cycle of abuse and foster a healthy and supportive partnership.

Abuse Tool: Rebuilding Trust.

It's essential to address the impact of past abuse in a relationship with sensitivity and care. When dealing with these issues, consider the following "Rebuilding Trust" tool to foster healing and support your partner:

Addressing past abuse in a relationship requires rebuilding trust, creating a safe space for healing, and fostering open communication. The following steps can contribute to rebuilding trust and supporting your partner:

Approach the topic with care and understanding. When problems arise, gently ask your partner if they are open to discussing their past. Allow them to share at their own pace.

If your partner has not shared their abusive past, avoid pressuring them. Respect their decision to keep it private, understanding they will share when ready and acknowledge your partner's feelings, even if it's not rational.

Create a safe space for your partner to share their thoughts and emotions. Listen without judgment, where they feel comfortable expressing themselves.

Refrain from minimizing or dismissing the significance of their past abuse. Give weight to their experiences, allow them to acknowledge and mourn their pain as part of the healing process and understand healing takes time, and there is no set endpoint, recognizing that it can be lengthy.

Celebrate your partner's small victories and positive steps in their healing journey. Acknowledge and appreciate moments of growth, comfort, and progress.

Sometimes, your partner needs someone to listen without judgment. Be there to provide emotional support and understanding, offering a listening ear when needed and recognize your own limitations and take care of your well-being throughout this process.

Building trust is a joint effort, and creating a robust and healthy relationship involves supporting each other through challenges. Whether you are a survivor or supporting a survivor, a compassionate and patient approach can contribute to overcoming difficulties and building a resilient partnership.

Forgiveness

When it comes to forgiveness in a partnership, it's essential to recognize the challenges that may arise and the transformative power of forgiveness in restoring harmony. Here are problems associated with forgiveness:

Some individuals believe that holding onto bitterness keeps their partners accountable for their actions. They may view anger and resentment as a form of justice. Holding onto these negative emotions can perpetuate a cycle of hurt and hinder true healing.

Conflicts within a partnership can trigger feelings of hurt and betrayal, intensifying pain and reopening past traumas. Forgiveness is complex process and requires introspection and a willingness to confront vulnerabilities.

The ego plays a significant role in forgiveness. When egos are bruised, making rational decisions and letting go of resentment becomes challenging. Hurt and vulnerability can activate ego-driven defense mechanisms that hinder the forgiveness process.

The belief that our partner doesn't deserve forgiveness because they hurt us may lead to a desire for vengeance. True forgiveness liberates us from this desire and encourages understanding of our partner's journey, including their pain, trauma, or experiences of abuse.

Embracing forgiveness requires recognizing the pain we've inflicted on others and our need for forgiveness. Acknowledging our own shortcomings cultivates empathy and creates a safe space for healing.

Forgiveness involves letting go of labels we assign to our partners, such as "evil" or "cruel." It encourages us to see them as complex individuals with their struggles and vulnerabilities.

The journey toward forgiveness may not be easy, but it is worth embarking on. It involves self-reflection, patience, and a commitment to growth. As partners learn to forgive, they can break free from bitterness and resentment, allowing love, compassion, and understanding to flourish in the relationship. The following pages will explore practical strategies and tools to cultivate forgiveness, heal wounds, and create a foundation of trust and harmony in relationships.

Forgiveness Tool: Don't Push Their Buttons

Their Buttons" is a proactive approach to healing within a partnership. The power of forgiveness lies in letting go of past hurts and creating a foundation for a healthier and more resilient relationship.
Here's a summary of the solution:

Solution: Embracing Forgiveness with "Don't Push Their Buttons"

Forgiveness is a potent tool for personal growth and strengthening the bond between partners. The key is to utilize the "Don't Push Their Buttons" tool, emphasizing mindfulness, respect for boundaries, and sensitivity to triggers. This approach creates a safe environment for healing and forgiveness.
Choosing to forgive is an act of strength that involves acknowledging past hurts, such as abuse or trauma, and finding the courage to move forward. By replacing bitterness with love, partners can open the door to healing and rediscover a profound connection.

The transformative power of forgiveness goes beyond rebuilding love; it can free individuals from negative patterns and contribute to a lasting legacy of love. The journey of forgiveness is also one of self-discovery and personal growth, enhancing self-esteem, inner strength, and a sense of safety and security.

Embracing forgiveness, coupled with the "Don't Push Their Buttons" tool, is a proactive and empowering approach to healing within a partnership. It allows individuals to let go of past hurts and establishes a foundation for a healthier and more resilient relationship.

Financial Secrets

Concealing financial secrets, such as maintaining hidden bank accounts, undisclosed loans, or engaging in economic activities without your partner's awareness, can lead to significant challenges in a relationship. It violates trust and boundaries, resulting in devastating consequences when the truth eventually surfaces. This form of deception is commonly known as financial infidelity, akin to a lie or betrayal that has the potential to cause irreparable damage to the relationship.

Many couples consider financial infidelity, encompassing the concealment of money or secret accounts, to be more detrimental than physical infidelity. Even seemingly minor actions, such as keeping silent about credit card debt or other financial secrets, contribute to this betrayal. The repercussions of hiding financial information can extend beyond simply concealing minor expenses or personal indulgences.

It is crucial to differentiate between managing personal finances and deliberately hiding them from your partner. Concealing money is an act of deception typically driven by fear, proving detrimental to the partnership. Consider whether the secrecy surrounding accounts stems from a lack of trust in your partner's financial responsibility or concerns about the relationship's longevity, possibly seeking a personal safety net.

People often resort to hiding money when underlying relationship issues exist, such as a lack of trust or commitment. The problem lies in maintaining financial secrets, among other things, failing to address these deeper issues or contribute to their resolution. Instead, it impedes the growth of a strong partnership.

Utilizing the tool "Financial Transparency" becomes imperative in addressing these challenges. This involves fostering open and honest communication about finances, sharing financial information, and making joint decisions regarding money matters. By promoting transparency and trust in your financial relationship, you can tackle underlying issues, seek solutions, and fortify your partnership.

Financial Secrets Tool: Transparency

Trust and open communication form the bedrock of a healthy relationship in a partnership. However, introducing hidden finances can undermine this foundation, leading to financial infidelity that profoundly impacts partners, leaving them feeling betrayed and questioning the integrity of their bond.

The issue arises when one partner engages in deceptive practices like concealing money, maintaining secret bank accounts, or withholding information about loans and credit card debt. These actions breach boundaries and erode trust, posing a significant threat to the stability of the partnership. Financial infidelity is often considered as detrimental, if not more so, than physical infidelity.

It's crucial to distinguish between managing personal finances and intentionally hiding them from a partner. The latter is a form of deception rooted in fear and insecurity, neither of which contributes positively to a thriving partnership. The underlying issues of trust and commitment often manifest in secret finances, where hiding money becomes a safeguard against potential financial irresponsibility or protection if the relationship falters.

To address this challenge and rebuild trust, partners must engage in open and honest dialogue about their financial practices. Defensive responses or attempts to justify past actions should be avoided, with a focus on understanding the underlying reasons behind the deception. Whether it's a perceived imbalance or addiction leading to damaging financial consequences, partners must secure their financial assets, seeking help for any addiction-related spending negatively impacting both parties' well-being. Decisions about shared finances should prioritize the best interests of both parties, ensuring a secure future together.

Recognizing that hidden finances often indicate more significant underlying issues like entitlement, shame, embarrassment, or worry, regular money check-ins should become a routine. These check-ins provide a dedicated space for openly discussing financial concerns and goals, fostering honesty and transparency. Partners can work together towards financial harmony.

By unraveling the web of hidden finances and embracing financial transparency, partners can strengthen their connections and a foundation for their shared future, and truly united in their financial journey.

Self Esteem/Insecurities

Let's talk about a common challenge in relationships – low self-esteem. In every partnership, it's natural to have some insecurities and areas for improvement. But when these insecurities hit hard and mess with your self-esteem, it can create a storm of emotions that ripples your relationship.

Dealing with low self-esteem isn't a passing phase; it's an ongoing battle. If you find yourself questioning your abilities, withdrawing from social situations, avoiding challenges, you might be in the midst of this internal struggle. It can mess with your mental health, leading to feelings of depression and anxiety. And it doesn't stop there – it can even make you doubt whether your partner truly loves you, wondering if they'd feel the same knowing your weaknesses.

Sometimes, you might do things you don't want to, to keep the relationship going. But if the balance tips and one partner is always taking without giving back, it can worsen your self-esteem, and harm the partnership.

Unhealthy relationships often bring in excessive criticism and judgment. Constant blame can make you feel flawed and unworthy, fostering jealousy and insecurity and even question your worth or fear your partner will leave.

It's crucial to prioritize building self-esteem and overcoming insecurities. Create an atmosphere of understanding and empathy with your partner, where criticism turns into constructive feedback, and judgment becomes compassion. Open and honest communication becomes the foundation for rebuilding self-esteem. Encourage each other to explore personal interests, take on new challenges, and celebrate achievements to reaffirm self-worth.

In partnerships, actively working on self-esteem and supporting each other's journey toward self-discovery and self-love is vital. Create an environment of emotional safety, understanding, and encouragement, navigating the complexities of low self-esteem together. Doing so will make you stronger and more resilient as a united front.

True love and partnership aren't about perfection; they're about accepting and cherishing each other's flaws and vulnerabilities. Embrace the journey of self-esteem building and overcoming insecurities as an opportunity for personal growth and deepening the bond that holds your partnership together

172

Self-Esteem/Insecurities Tool: Empowerment

The tool for Sel-Estem is Empowerment.

Look, we all have aspects we'd like to improve – a few insecurities are part of the human experience. However, when these insecurities become deep-rooted, they can create a continuous struggle, affecting not just your inner feelings but also the dynamics of your partnership.

Dealing with low self-esteem is more than a fleeting challenge; it's an ongoing battle that can make you question your abilities, withdraw from social situations, and impact your mental health. A partnership can cast doubts on your worthiness of love and lead you to ask if your partner would genuinely love you with all your vulnerabilities. This may push you to do things you don't genuinely desire, upsetting the balance in the relationship.

Unhealthy partnerships involve excessive criticism and judgment, feelings of shame and worsening low self-esteem. Feeling flawed can trigger jealousy and insecurity, with doubts about your worthiness and fear of abandonment.

If your partner struggles with self-esteem, understand how you can offer support. Regular communication is crucial for them to feel secure. Empowering your partner by celebrating their achievements, big or small, and sharing these with friends and family strengthens the partnership.

Remember, the world can be harsh, and those with similar insecurities may try to take advantage, but these shortcomings often hold little significance to others. It's essential to separate self-imposed doubts and fears from the reality. In moments of attacks on self-esteem, trust that your partner will protect you. Making your partner the most essential thing in your life.

Building self-esteem and overcoming insecurities is a journey. With open communication, support, and a deep understanding of the value you bring to the partnership, you and your partner can foster a strong and nurturing bond. You have the power to make a difference and create a partnership that thrives on love, respect, and belief in each other's strengths.

All These
Things Affect
Trust

Money Issues
Family
White Lies
Withholding Information

GONZALO

Chapter 10:
Daily Tools for Relationship Trust

Boundaries

It's not a lack of love but a lack of trust that creates an unhappy partnership. When does the unhappiness reach a point where prioritizing love and integrity with your partner becomes essential, aiming for 100 percent trust? When does the discontent with deception lead to a readiness for honesty, even if the response is unfavorable? When does the burden of stress prompt a commitment to keeping your word without excuses? When does the weight of guilt become the catalyst for honest self-reflection, moving beyond blaming your partner for a strained relationship? When do these realizations culminate to take ownership of the future of your partnership and, more importantly, transform it for the better?

Healthy partnerships rely on well-defined boundaries. These boundaries establish your comfort level and the treatment you expect from your partner. As you've witnessed, boundaries are pivotal in almost every aspect of a thriving relationship. Respecting your partner's boundaries and assisting them in respecting yours is the key to a happy life. Crossing these boundaries only complicates life unnecessarily.

Violating boundaries undermines trust in a partnership. Such violations manifest in various forms, from disregarding personal space, family, friends, and privacy to intruding on finances, beliefs, and health status. Many partners have never openly discussed or acknowledged each other's boundary issues, so make it a point to now understand your partner's boundaries.

Attempting to change your partner or relying on outsiders to solve problems is crossing a line. Resorting to threats or intimidation also constitutes crossing a line. Taking advantage or causing harm, is another boundary breach.

Moving your partner's belongings without consent or snooping through their phone, mail, and emails without permission crosses a line. Taking pictures of your partner against their wishes or posting comments/images on social media without consent is a violation. Consuming their food without asking or occupying their usual spot on the couch similarly represents a boundary breach.

Crossing boundaries is a sign of disrespect. If this is happening, it's OK to own it and to say, "You're right, I'm wrong."

Boundaries Tool: Think Before You Act

Establishing boundaries is paramount for a healthy partnership. Reflect on your relationship—do you believe it embodies healthiness? Is your partner comfortable sharing everything, confident that their boundaries will be respected? If there's a history of oversharing and boundary violations, it's time to employ the "Think Before You Act" tool.

Approach your partnership with a fresh mindset, akin to when you first met. Assume you don't know each other's boundaries or motivations, so now ask. This exercise demonstrates love, hope, and care for the partnership.

Begin by jotting down your boundaries—financial, intellectual, physical, emotional, or sexual. Identify actions that would make you feel violated. Have your partner create their list, and exchange notes. Are you aware of these boundaries? Understanding what is mutually agreeable and unacceptable.

The second part of "Think Before You Act" involves expressing your readiness to be a better partner, emphasizing improved boundary respect. When communicating feelings or philosophies, use "we" instead of "I" statements. Avoid starting sentences with "you always" or "you never," and refrain from making ultimatums. Remember, you're not negotiating with an enemy.

Address family dynamics by setting boundaries to protect each other from external pressures without guilt. Apply similar rules to friendships—establish mutual boundaries and respect personal space. If you've isolated your partner from friends, reset boundaries and determine the justification.

Discuss goals and dreams openly. Unless a partner's pursuit directly impacts the other, set mutual boundaries on spending related to such endeavors. Allow space for individual dreams that don't affect the relationship negatively.

Address sexual boundaries. Be open to experimentation within agreed-safe and secure limits. Communication is key in setting these boundaries set.

Revisit the topic of flirting and set a rule: if it can be done in front of your partner is ok with it, it's acceptable. If you find yourself waiting until your partner leaves the room, recognize that a boundary has been crossed. Becoming a master at respecting boundaries is a vital component in creating a happy, healthy, and fulfilling partnership. Strive to be that overachiever.

Integrity

It's not a lack of love, but a lack of trust
that creates an unhappy partnership

Integrity is a foundational element in a robust partnership, embodying honesty, moral principles, and moral uprightness. It involves fulfilling commitments and forms the basis of trust and reliability. A lack of integrity, manifested in breaking promises of patience, kindness, understanding, and love, can significantly impact relationships, undermining the trust pillar.

The issue of keeping secrets is intricately tied to trust in a relationship. While recognizing the occasional need for confidentiality, charging partners believe that keeping secrets is ultimately in the best interest of both individuals.

Even the most compassionate individuals may grapple with making morally right choices in challenging situations, leading to an internal struggle between conflicting influences.

Self-integrity emphasizes aligning personal actions and choices with ethical standards. It reflects the commitment to moral principles in one's conduct.

Relationship integrity spans various journey stages, including friendship, gentleness, mutual acceptance of influence, and shared fondness and admiration. These stages contribute to the development of lasting and stable relationships.

If flaws in a relationship stem from a lack of integrity, it's crucial to acknowledge the issue. The choice lies in either working towards restoring the goodness within the relationship or, if necessary, gradually disengaging for personal well-being.

Recognizing that integrity can be tested and may cross boundaries within a partnership is crucial. In such cases, the importance of acknowledging the situation and embracing the phrase, "You're right, I'm wrong," is emphasized. This fosters open communication and facilitates conflict resolution.

Integrity Tool: Transparency.

As an exemplary partner, integrity should be a fundamental principle guiding your actions. It necessitates honesty, truthfulness, and reliability, fostering a relationship where your partner can trust your word.

Transparency, as a tool, plays a vital role in maintaining integrity. Secrets can significantly impact integrity, eroding trust. While privacy is natural, transparency about critical matters affecting your partner is essential.

Demonstrating integrity involves staying true to promises, whether simple tasks like household chores or more significant responsibilities like joint ventures. By consistently honoring commitments, you build trust.

Compromise is a crucial aspect of being a great partner. Recognize that meeting every demand might not always be feasible, communicate openly with your partner to find collaborative solutions. Instead of making empty promises or postponing tasks, express limitations and ensure follow-through.

This includes openness about significant financial decisions, debts, or any information with potential repercussions for the partnership. Financial honesty, in particular, is crucial to avoid damage, so maintaining openness about money matters and refraining from hiding or lying is paramount.

Resist the temptation to tell white lies, as it can set the stage for a slippery slope of deception. Even small dishonesties can undermine trust and weaken the foundation of your partnership. Upholding integrity ensures your partner feels secure and confident in the relationship, knowing they can rely on your honorable and responsible actions during crises or stressful situations.

Addressing any hidden secrets related to addictions is critical. Openness and honesty about these struggles are vital for the well-being of individuals and the partnership. Acknowledging and confronting these challenges can foster a stronger, more supportive relationship.

Remember, as a great partner, maintaining integrity brings balance, equality, and security, ultimately rebuilding trust within the partnership. By staying true to your word, being open and honest, and addressing hidden secrets, you demonstrate your unwavering commitment to the principles of integrity, creating a solid foundation for a thriving partnership.

Intimacy

The secret to a happy and long partnership is not keeping emotional distance

The problem section on intimacy adeptly identifies various interconnected factors that contribute to a lack of intimacy in a relationship. It recognizes the multifaceted nature of the issue, encompassing communication challenges, mental health issues, resentment, external demands, and more. The acknowledgment that the impact extends beyond the physical aspect, affecting the trust pillar, adds depth to the understanding of the issue.

The mention of stress as a potential hindrance to intimacy, creating emotional distance and reducing the desire for connection, resonates with the complexities that external pressures can introduce. The incorporation of mental health conditions, such as depression, and their influence on sexual desire and intimacy provides a nuanced perspective on the topic.

The consideration of varying levels of sexual desire between partners and the potential effects of hormonal changes due to stress on libido contributes to a comprehensive examination of intimacy challenges. Additionally, the recognition of the lasting effects of past experiences of sexual abuse on a person's ability to engage in healthy sexual relationships emphasizes the importance of addressing underlying trauma.

The section effectively emphasizes the significance of open and respectful communication, viewing each other as equals, and discussing values to ensure alignment and understanding in building a happy relationship. The mention of conflicts being normal but the importance of mature handling signifies a realistic approach to relationship dynamics.

Finally, the recognition of the vital importance of addressing the lack of intimacy in maintaining a solid partnership and the emphasis on humility and willingness to admit fault contribute to a well-rounded understanding of the problem at hand. Overall, the section provides a comprehensive overview of the factors contributing to intimacy issues and sets the stage for exploring potential solutions.

Intimacy Tool: Connection

Physical touch, such as holding hands, hugging, and gentle touching, triggers a chemical reaction in our brains, creating a calming sensation. Surprisingly, our brains experience heightened pleasure when the anticipation of a reward lingers before it is received. Therefore, take your time during foreplay, allowing the tension to build.

Additionally, it is essential to separate sexual intimacy from routine. Avoid discussing relationship problems and chores in the bedroom. Plan dedicated time for intimacy and explore various activities that pleasure both partners. Enjoy the courting process and embrace flirting as a way to reignite sexual desire and intimacy. Carve out quality time to spend with your partner.

Remember that foreplay does not always have to lead to sexual intercourse. Affectionate touch is a powerful way to demonstrate and rekindle passion, even for those who may not naturally be touchy-feely. Focus on fostering loving touch and practice being emotionally vulnerable during sex. Share your deepest wishes, fantasies, and desires while considering your partner's needs gently and lovingly. If it has been a while, take it slow and infuse romance into your interactions—plan a special dinner, watch a movie together, and savor the moments.

Finally, change your approach to initiating sex. Flirt with and kiss your partner. Discover their erogenous zones and make it happen! If you have specific desires or fantasies, communicate them openly and encourage your partner to do the same. Remember, maintaining a healthy level of emotional and physical intimacy requires effort, communication, and a commitment to prioritize your partner's satisfaction.

The tool of "Intimate Connection" serves as a guide to help partners rekindle the flame of intimacy by incorporating thoughtful gestures, affectionate touch, and open communication. By actively engaging in these practices, couples can create a fulfilling and harmonious partnership that celebrates the beauty of both emotional and physical connection.

Lifestyle

Life is a hard hat zone— always under construction.

When partners live different lifestyles, it can lead to a variety of challenges within the relationship. Differences in wishes, beliefs, and ideas about various aspects of life, such as where to live, work-life balance, spending habits, travel preferences, and decisions about having children, can create friction. The key is to these differences is to ensure a harmonious partnership.

The problem arises when partners are not aligned, and one partner's viewpoint dominates the relationship. This imbalance can make the other partner feel invisible, leading to a sense of loss in identity, vision, and dreams, ultimately jeopardizing the partnership. Companionship, compatibility, genuine love, shared history, and a deep understanding of each other are fundamental elements that people value in a partnership. When these critical components undergo changes or are missing, problems arise.

For example, if one partner becomes a couch potato while the other still enjoys socializing and traveling, a disconnect may occur. It's essential to find common ground and solutions that address these differences without allowing negative behavior, such as an attitude of superiority or disrespect, to emerge.

Navigating different lifestyles requires open communication, understanding, and a willingness to compromise. Partners should actively engage in discussions about their individual preferences and work together to find middle ground that satisfies both. Finding shared activities and interests can help bridge the gap between different lifestyles and strengthen the bond between partners.

In moments of disagreement or when facing lifestyle-related challenges, it's crucial to approach the situation with empathy and a genuine desire to understand your partner's perspective. Building a partnership that accommodates and respects each other's individuality contributes to a healthy and fulfilling relationship. Remember, the goal is not necessarily to agree on everything but to find solutions that honor both partners' needs.

Don't let differences in lifestyles create contempt. If you have done this, it's OK to own it and to say, "You're right, I'm wrong.

Lifestyle Tool: Attitude Adjustment

When navigating different lifestyles in a partnership, it's crucial to embrace each other's differences and cultivate an attitude of acceptance and respect. The tool for achieving this is "Attitude Adjustment." Instead of attempting to change or control your partner to conform to your preferences, focus on accepting them for who they are and taking an interest in their viewpoint.

Attitude Adjustment involves refraining from shaming your partner for their lifestyle choices. If there are aspects that you find challenging or disagreeable, practice a cool-down period before expressing any negative comments. It's essential to recognize and respect your partner's autonomy, allowing them to be themselves without unnecessary criticism.

Another aspect of Attitude Adjustment is building admiration for your partner's differences. Find ways to praise and appreciate the unique qualities that make them who they are. Even if you don't adopt those differences in your own actions, show support and understanding. For instance, if your partner enjoys certain foods that you dislike, consider ordering those for them without making negative comments.

Skills learned in Chapter 4, such as asking questions and assessing how you address issues with your partner, complement the Attitude Adjustment approach. In moments of disagreement or annoyance, pause, compromise, and let go of the need to control or change your partner.

This tool helps you keep your emotions in check and conveys messages such as "I love you as you are" and "I'm not trying to change you."

Attitude Adjustment encourages a mindset of equality, acknowledging that both partners have the right to make choices that align with their preferences. It emphasizes open communication without trying to exert control. By picking your battles wisely and respecting each other's autonomy, you contribute to a stronger and more harmonious partnership. Remember, the goal is not to make your partner exactly like you but to appreciate and support each other's individuality.

Relationship Dynamics

A perfect partnership is just two imperfect people
who refuse to give up on each other

In any partnership, aligning values and maintaining open communication are essential for navigating the challenges that arise from relationship differences. As individuals and as a couple, you will undergo changes over time, raising the crucial question of whether you choose to change together. It is imperative to do so to ensure the trust pillar of your partnership, underscoring the significance of being on the same page.

Beyond personal changes, various factors can influence relationship dynamics. Relationships experience different developmental stages and are influenced by events such as job loss, health problems, financial issues, and family conflict. These circumstances act as natural catalysts for change, emphasizing the need to anticipate and address them as a partnership.

Small changes may occur, such as one partner becoming less tidy or dedicating more time to personal interests. Challenges arise when your partner's behavior diverges from its previous state, showing a different level of interest in spending time together.

Significant changes, however, can be even more challenging to navigate, directly conflicting with your thoughts or values. For instance, your partner may change their mind about wanting children, or their preference for an urban lifestyle may clash with your shared dream of raising kids in a rural area. Differences in political beliefs or a shift in career aspirations, like your partner wanting to transition from being a CEO to becoming a teacher, can also pose substantial challenges.

It's crucial to acknowledge that your partner is constantly evolving. Failing to make a deliberate effort to connect regularly can lead to growing apart, waking up one day feeling like you're with a stranger. Creating rituals integral to your shared life can help you grow together and foster fond memories.

If your partner's changes become overwhelming, it's time to approach the situation differently. The book can be instrumental in this regard, encouraging asking questions to understand your partner's differences, making supportive choices, be willing to compromise to find common ground. Communication is crucial in navigating these dynamics and fostering understanding.

Relationship Dynamics Tool: Ownership

Relationships go through various stages and situations, including challenges like job loss, health problems, financial issues, and family conflicts. It's natural for changes to occur within a partnership, leading to differences in opinions, beliefs, and values. When one partner actively seeks change, discussion, and resolution to relationship issues, while the other partner withdraws and avoids addressing them, it's crucial to prioritize effective communication and understanding.

In such situations, focusing more on listening to your partner's perspective is essential rather than solely expressing your own. Take the initiative to initiate conversations after disagreements, be willing to apologize when necessary, and recognize that your partner's anger may stem from hurt or fear rather than hatred toward you. When your partner expresses anger, they are actually fighting for the relationship, and it's important to acknowledge their emotions and support them.

Partnerships involve continuous personal growth and change. However, if your partner's changes become too overwhelming or contradictory to your thoughts and values, it's time to approach the situation differently. The book provides tools to understand and address your partner's differences, make choices that support them, and find compromises to align your perspectives. Above all, effective communication plays a vital role in understanding and resolving relationship dynamics.

Relationship dynamics can sometimes cross boundaries, affecting the trust pillar of the partnership. In such instances, it's crucial to adopt a mindset of "You're Right, I'm Wrong" and work towards finding common ground and mutual understanding. Open and honest communication allows both partners to express their needs, concerns, and boundaries, fostering a healthier and more balanced partnership.

To maintain a solid and connected partnership, it's essential to actively engage with your partner regularly. Create rituals and shared activities that become a part of your life together, fostering fond memories and growth. Remember, the partnership is a journey of continuous change, and making a deliberate effort to connect and understand each other will help you grow together rather than apart. Nurturing the relationship with intention, curiosity, and love ensures that both partners feel seen, valued, and supported throughout all seasons of life.

Second Guessing

If I did anything right in my life, it was choosing you.

Even in the healthiest partnerships, doubt can sneak in—not through major conflicts, but in subtle, persistent moments of second-guessing.

Do you find yourself questioning how your partner handles things? Offering your opinion, only to watch them choose a different path? These situations may seem minor, but they often reflect deeper issues—such as a lack of trust, the need for control, or fear of letting go.

Second-guessing can arise from diminished confidence—either in your partner or the relationship itself. And when trust fades, emotional safety disappears. What once was support turns into scrutiny. What once felt like teamwork begins to feel like performance.

Trust is foundational. Without it, it's natural to feel disconnected, unsupported, and unsure. But when you have confidence in your partner's ability to make decisions, you create space for the relationship to grow and thrive.

Decisions shouldn't be made in silos. Shutting each other out leads to distance and potential resentment. Real partnership is built on mutual respect, open dialogue, and compromise.

And if you've fallen into a habit of second-guessing, it's okay to own it. Sometimes the most powerful thing you can say is:
"You're right. I'm wrong."

Not as surrender, but as a step toward trust, understanding, and stronger connection.

Second Guessing Tool: Think It, Don't Say It

When you know someone so well, including shortcomings, second-guessing is second nature. It happens more than we want to admit. It's like having inside information on your partner, and it can be unfair at times. Anything you say or do will be used against you in the court of your own house.

Think It, Don't Say It is the Tool, be OK when your partner doesn't make what you think is the best decision for the health of the partnership. Stop second-guessing your partner and work toward being more aligned.

Adopt a give-and-take strategy, allowing your partner to make decisions without criticism, the same done for you. Tthis can only happen through communication and compromise. Let your partner do it their way, even if you disagree. The results might surprise you if you Think It, Don't Say It. If it didn't work for the best, make suggestions for future situations and move on.

LET YOUR PARTNER MAKE THE NEXT MAJOR DECISION. LET THEM MAKE IT WITHOUT QUESTIONING OR JUDGMENT.

Life can be easier if you know why your partner makes their decisions. All you need to do is ask. Talking it out is the key to agreeing or disagreeing with your partner without criticism. As a partnership, you should be able to understand and support one another without an argument or resorting to anything resembling 'how dare you question my actions.' Those misunderstandings stem from miscommunication. When you jump to conclusions about what you think you know, and what your partner is thinking, you end up in misery. You're not a mind reader. Ask the question!

It's human nature to think you have all the answers—your way is the only way. But sometimes your partner can have a better way. Suppose you'd just let them have it. Don't push your opinion; just go with theirs. If they're wrong, don't judge them or rub it in their face as though you never made a mistake before. Get in the habit of implementing Think It, Don't Say It."

Ask yourself, If I had to do it over, what would I do it differently? There is such a thing as grace in just saying, "You're right, I'm wrong."

Technology

When you live your life as an open book
your partner can read from your pages

Technology has undoubtedly transformed our lives, including how we interact and communicate within relationships. However, it also brings challenges and problems that can negatively impact partnerships.

One significant issue is the excessive use of technology, where individuals prioritize their phones, TVs, or computers over their partners. This behavior can create stress, diminish affection, and make partners feel unappreciated. It can lead to conflict, dissatisfaction, and even demise the relationship.

The influence of social media on relationships must be considered. Spending excessive time on platforms like Facebook or Instagram before bed can foster jealousy and communication issues. In fact, social media has become a leading cause of significant problems within partnerships. Excessive reliance on social media can undermine face-to-face interaction, reducing communication time and intimacy, which can have long-term consequences.

The prevalence of online gaming can also pose a threat to relationships. Spending excessive time immersed in virtual reality can lead to neglecting real-life interactions and responsibilities. Partners may feel ignored or disconnected as the virtual world consumes their significant other.

Additionally, technology can distort connections between partners. Excessive texting, for example, may erode the intimacy of hearing each other's voices and engaging in meaningful conversations. Finding a balance essential.

It's essential to recognize that technology has the potential to cross boundaries. This book aims to help navigate these challenges, emphasizing humility and the willingness to admit when one partner may be wrong.

Finding a balance between technology and personal connections is crucial for a healthy and thriving partnership. Recognizing the impact of excessive technology use, openly communicating about its effects, and intentionally prioritizing quality time together can help mitigate the problems caused by technology and foster a stronger bond between partners.

Technology Tool: Open Book

Addressing these concerns is essential if you find that technology is causing issues in your partnership, such as spending excessive time on your phone, TV, computer, or gaming. Overindulgence in technology can create stress, diminish affection, and make your partner feel unappreciated. Consider implementing the 'Open Book' tool to prevent further conflict and dissatisfaction.

If your partner has concerns about your trustworthiness due to questionable content on social media or private texts, it's crucial to rebuild trust. The 'Open Book' tool allows you to become more transparent, providing your partner access to your emails and phone if they request it. By offering this level of transparency, you can alleviate their trust and stress issues, fostering a sense of security in the partnership.

Recognize when your excessive use of technology triggers your partner's insecurities, and utilize the 'Open Book' tool to reconnect with them. By granting your partner access to your digital devices, you demonstrate your commitment to the relationship's well-being and peace of mind. Remember, prioritizing your partner's trust and safety outweighs privacy concerns.

Regular communication and open dialogue are essential in resolving technology-related conflicts. Ask your partner how you can improve, and seek ways to be more present and attentive. Additionally, positively leverage technology by using online shared calendars to stay organized and minimize expectations. Explore apps that recommend date night activities and utilize YouTube tutorials to learn new skills or complete tasks together. These actions demonstrate your commitment, love, respect, and care as a partner.

Excessive technology use can lead to jealousy and communication breakdowns in a partnership. Maintain transparency with your partner and prioritize their sense of security and trust. Remember, being an 'Open Book' creates a game-changing dynamic in the relationship, fostering a stronger bond.

By implementing these solutions and embracing the 'Open Book' tool, you can alleviate the negative impacts of technology, rebuild trust, and create a more harmonious and connected partnership.

White Lies

Be that person who ruins your partner's lipstick,
not their mascara.

A white lie becomes hazardous when used to protect your hide. It's hard to imagine how a little lie can get so out of hand, but it can. The issue with the little white lie is that it may start your partner thinking about what other lies they missed.

An often-overlooked consequence of lying is that your partner's trust is violated. It's not that they haven't been lied to in the past. It's that they were lied to by you. You are supposed to be the only one in their life that they should be able to count on. They now feel betrayed and angry. Now that their eyes are wide open, it's only human for them to revisit the past to see what else they missed. In this web of suspicion, they can't help but feel foolish, even humiliated.

Understand that your partnership is now treading on betrayal issues everywhere. Lies and trust cannot easily coexist. Lying will eventually shatter confidence.

The first time your partner uncovers a white lie, it's not hard to understand that they will question everything you say or do until the trust is built back up. When are you coming home? Where did you go? Who were you with? What did you do? You might even catch your partner looking at your texts or emails when you're not around. You must understand that you lost your privacy because you got caught lying. You have no one to blame but you.

The more you lie, the more your partner will protect themselves. They'll add another brick to that wall until there's no way for you to get through, over, or around.

White lies can build walls between partners. If this happens, it's OK to own it and say, "You're right, I'm wrong."

190

White Lies Tool: Honesty

Oh! That harmless little white lie. Fibbing is just in our DNA. You know those little ones we mastered as kids to get what we wanted TO never be denied.

When your mother said you could go out and play after your homework was done, you answered, "My homework's done!" It wasn't. Then we got older and saved leftover cash to bet on a game even though we told our partner we were done gambling. "I've quit smoking—this is my last cigarette!" you say and mean it until you end up having a stressful day, taking your willpower out the window along with your promise. That's when you need to kick in some Honesty.

Honesty as a skill says two things: do what you say you're going to do, and don't commit to something you're not ready to do. It does not say that you have to reveal every personal thought you might have. You can be private about your beliefs but not the actions that affect your partnership.

CAN YOU JUST OWN IT? THE NEXT TIME YOU DON'T WANT TO DEAL WITH THE CRAP, JUST BE HONEST WITH THE WHITE LIE AND LET INTEGRITY LIVE.

Do you know how to tell when you've crossed a line? It's when you justify your lies and find yourself going to extremes to keep them private. You can even feel that it is wrong when you're doing it.

What happens when you show up late for work regularly? They fire you because they can't count on you. It's the same deal when you get reamed because you told your partner you would be there at a specific time and were late. Why? Because they can't trust or count on you. You've heard it before. Your partner has said they can't trust you because...

Diplomacy is not a white lie. It's okay to answer personal questions with thoughtful honesty, setting boundaries without being deceptive. Saying something like, 'I'm not ready to talk about that yet,' is more respectful and trustworthy than offering a sugar-coated half-truth. True intimacy thrives on honesty delivered with care.

TRUST PILLAR

Abandonment

Deception

Double Life

Emotionally Disconnected

Baggage Issue
Tools to Repair
The Trust Pillar

Unresolved problems that one or both partners
bring into the relationship.

Abandoment

Abandonment fears can significantly impact your partner's ability to trust you, making it harder for them to feel worthy or intimate in the relationship. When one partner suffers from historical abandonment issues, it can manifest in various ways, affecting the partnership dynamics. They may act withdrawn, exhibit jealousy, or accuse you of being cold and distant, making you feel responsible for hurting them. It is essential to recognize that their behavior stems from their fear of being abandoned again.

One common coping mechanism for abandonment issues is disengagement. They may constantly strive to please you and give excessively in the relationship, hoping to prevent rejection and insecurity. However, this can lead to an imbalance where they feel they are giving too much, which can strain the partnership.

Individuals who fear abandonment can also have smothering behavior and become anxious when apart from their partner. They may try to prevent their partner from seeing family or friends because they want to be the sole focus of their partner. On the other hand, they may also struggle with holding on and not fully engaging in the relationship, fearing eventual abandonment.

When partners find themselves with varying interests, work schedules, or sleep patterns, it can trigger feelings of abandonment for one or both individuals. It becomes imperative to invest additional effort in spending quality time together to maintain the relationship's vibrancy and vitality. Take a moment to reflect on whether the fear of abandonment has influenced engaging in overly dependent or people-pleasing behaviors.

In social situations, you may withdraw for protection or feel vulnerable due to abandonment fears. These challenges can strain the partnership and hinder open communication and emotional connection. It's essential to address these issues through open and honest conversations.

Understanding and supporting your partner through abandonment issues requires patience, empathy, and clear communication. By working together and acknowledging the impact of these issues on the partnership, you can build trust, establish healthy boundaries, and foster a solid and secure bond.

Abandonment Tool: Kid Gloves

Understanding that your partner grapples with abandonment issues is crucial. They may have developed a defense mechanism of pushing people away, especially when feeling challenged or vulnerable, particularly in relation to you. If you choose to navigate through this, it's important to remain calm during conversations and avoid pressuring for immediate answers. Allow your partner the space and time they need to open up, and show them that you can be trusted.

Using the "KID GLOVES" tool means handling the situation with sensitivity, understanding, and non-judgment. If your partner is suddenly experiencing abandonment issues, create an opportunity to spend quality time together and gently approach the topic. Let your partner relax in your presence and reassure them that you can handle this issue. Building trust in addressing abandonment issues is a significant step in strengthening the partnership.

Love and support are vital during these challenging times. Provide a safe space for your partner to express their anxiety and fears without judgment. By understanding their pain and struggles, you can better comprehend their experiences and find ways to support their healing journey with positivity and encouragement. Use the "KID GLOVES" tool to ease their concerns and alleviate their pain.

Due to the fear of abandonment, your partner may display manipulative behaviors during intense conversations or arguments. At times, rationality may feel impossible for them. Take extra steps to ensure your partner feels your unwavering presence and support. It's important to recognize that their actions are not a response to anything you have done. They are following patterns established when they experienced trauma, attempting to avoid being hurt again. After an emotional outburst, it's a great opportunity to continue the conversation and explore the underlying issues.

Remember, healing from abandonment issues is a process that requires patience, understanding, and compassion. Be there for your partner, listen attentively, and validate their emotions. Encourage them to seek professional help if necessary and be their unwavering pillar of support. Together, you can navigate through these challenges and strengthen your bond as a partnership built on trust, love, and resilience.

Deception

Deception within a partnership creates significant challenges and can have lasting adverse effects. Are you lying to your partner, hiding secrets such as addiction, financial issues, mistakes, leading a double life, or driven by the fear of rejection or losing them?

When deception occurs, in some cases, they can be unforgivable, particularly within a partnership. Lying is a common transgression that can cause immense damage, second only to pride. The result is a state of paranoia, as the constant effort to maintain the façade raises doubts about everything.

Lying tears apart partnerships, friendships, and families, and lives can be devastated by the weight of that one small word: "lie."

Deception erodes the four pillars that uphold a healthy partnership: balance, equality, security, and trust. It breeds an atmosphere of deceit and selfishness, leading to a profound betrayal of the relationship is foundation. Discovering lies can inflict immense pain, challenging healing and rebuilding trust.

No matter how adept you think you are at concealing things, the truth can emerge. Partners often piece together clues, unraveling the web of deception. Burying deceit within destroys the purity of the relationship. However, one thing remains certain: when lies occur, a life of genuine happiness becomes unattainable, as guilt weighs heavily upon the one who lies.

Recognize the gravity of the situation and understand that the moment your partner discovers they have been deceived, it will be one of the most painful experiences they have ever gone through.

Deception Tool: It Hurts

To address deception within the partnership, embracing honesty, vulnerability, and open communication is essential. Recognize the gravity of the damage caused by deceit and commit to rebuilding trust through transparency and genuine remorse. Rebuilding a partnership after deception requires patience, forgiveness, and a mutual commitment to rebuilding the shattered trust. it is crucial to put an end to the lies and the behaviors associated with them. This is where the "IT HURTS" tool comes into play. It's time to apply all the tools mentioned in the disconnect and double life sections to prevent the devastating consequences of deception from becoming a reality.

Remember, trust is the cornerstone of a strong partnership. You create an environment where love, respect, and security can flourish by upholding honesty and transparency. Together, with open hearts and sincere efforts, you can overcome the challenges posed by deception and nurture a partnership grounded in truth and authenticity.

Rebuilding trust requires consistent and open communication. Be willing to have difficult conversations, address past deceptions, and take responsibility for your actions. Show genuine remorse and demonstrate your commitment to change. Understanding that rebuilding trust takes both partners' time, patience, and consistent effort.

Remember, the goal is to create a foundation of trust built on honesty, openness, and integrity. By stopping the deception and committing to a path of truthfulness, you can work towards healing and creating a stronger, more authentic partnership.

Disconnected

At some point in every relationship, you may experience a sense of being "disconnected" from your partner. This can occur when you've been preoccupied with work or other obligations, resulting in limited quality time together. You may feel a noticeable emotional distance, a sense that something is amiss. Your partner may have become nothing more than a distant roommate, and this disconnection triggers a cascade of negative consequences. In such moments, you may question the foundation of your relationship, wondering where the fun and joy have gone. When a disconnect sets in, love, excitement, and fulfillment fade.

When a partner becomes emotionally disconnected, it gives rise to several problems within the partnership. Engaging in a one-sided partnership can be draining, leaving you with a sense of indifference. Misunderstandings become commonplace, patience wears thin, and a pervasive feeling of exhaustion permeates the relationship. Conversations with your partner lose their pleasantness, burdening you with a heavy sense of loneliness and negative energy. Intimacy fades away, and online pornography may replace the emotional and physical connection that once existed.

Intimacy fades away, and online pornography may replace the emotional and physical connection that once existed. While this may be harmless if your partner is comfortable with it, if they are not, it can be perceived as a form of infidelity. When a relationship lacks physical, psychological, and emotional intimacy, it clearly indicates that the partnership is failing.

Additionally, the lack of emotional connection may lead to a breakdown in communication, further deepening the sense of isolation between partners. Trust issues may arise as partners feel neglected and unimportant. The absence of shared experiences and quality time together can create a growing emotional gap that becomes challenging to bridge. This emotional disconnection can also impact the overall satisfaction and fulfillment within the relationship, leaving both partners feeling unfulfilled and dissatisfied.

Disconnected Tool: Reinvest

Now, let's explore solutions to fix a totally disconnected partner, it's the REINVEST" tool . Although it may feel like your relationship is falling apart right now, it's important to remember that it's not necessarily the end. Instead, it's a sign that it's time to take a different approach.

Take the time to genuinely understand why your partner feels disconnected. Try to see things from their perspective and resist becoming defensive. Open up and explain your own feelings and intentions as well. Show empathy towards your partner and dig deeper into the underlying issues.

Engage in open and honest communication with your partner. Discuss the reasons for the emotional disconnect and explore any underlying concerns. Encourage your partner to express their feelings and concerns, and be willing to actively listen without judgment.

Disconnections often stem from deeper issues. Explore the root causes of the emotional distance and work together to address these issues. This may involve seeking professional help, such as couples therapy, to navigate complex emotions and find practical solutions.

If trust has been eroded during the disconnection, commit to rebuilding it. This involves consistent and open communication, genuine remorse, and concrete actions to restore confidence.

Make a conscious effort to spend quality time together. Rediscover shared activities and hobbies that brought joy to the relationship. Prioritize intimacy and emotional connection, gradually rebuilding the sense of closeness that may have diminished.

Approach the process with a positive attitude and a genuine commitment to making positive changes. Acknowledge the issues, take responsibility for your part, and actively work towards creating a more connected and fulfilling partnership.

Remember, it's not your fault for a strained partnership; now you can prove it. By applying the knowledge and tools you have acquired, your partner will likely respond positively. Your partner needs to feel secure, rebuild trust, and know that you genuinely want them back in your life.

Double Life

Living a double life can create significant problems within a partnership, which may arise from various underlying reasons. One partner might feel unfulfilled in meeting their needs, self-sabotage due to a lack of self-worth, find excitement in maintaining a massive secret, struggle to integrate conflicting aspects of their personality, or desire to live out a fantasy separate from their primary partner.

Signs that your partner may be leading a double life include changes in spending habits, the secrecy surrounding financial matters, shifts in personality and behaviors, alterations in clothing or self-care patterns, excessive time spent on the computer, frequent trips away from home, late-night calls or texts with flirtatious undertones, unfamiliar smells, intuition, difficulty remembering events or anniversaries, and noticeable irritability when discussing personal or family circumstances.

In the age of social media, individuals often present an idealized version of themselves, concealing struggles and portraying a glamorous front to their partner, friends, family, and the world. This illusion of financial success or overall well-being can be maintained even when the reality is far from it. Addictions, primarily, provide a breeding ground for leading a double life and hiding secrets. Those struggling with addiction become adept at concealing their destructive habits, going to great lengths to avoid revealing the truth.

Online gambling has made it easier for individuals to lead double lives as gamblers without their partners suspecting. Gamblers become masters of deception, hiding their addiction and maintaining a facade of normalcy.
One crucial indicator that something is amiss is your gut feeling. Often dismissed or rationalized, trusting your instincts is vital. Pay attention to subtle signs, such as a tightening in your stomach when a lie is being told or a sense of emotional disconnection from your partner.

Addressing the issue of a double life in a partnership requires open and honest communication. If you suspect or have evidence of your partner's deception, it is crucial to confront the situation with care and seek professional help if needed. Building trust and authenticity is vital for a healthy and fulfilling partnership.

Double Life Tool: WTF

It's crucial to address and resolve the issue of living a double life to rebuild trust and mend the damaged bridge in your partnership. The tool to fix this is the WTF tool.

Recognize the power of secret lives and the potential harm they can cause. Living a double life means adhering to different rules and codes of conduct, motivated by different needs than those portrayed to the world. However, this duality undermines the trust you promised your partner. It's time to put an end to it and make things right. If the situation has escalated to this point, your bridge is severely damaged and needs to be repaired before it collapses.

Ending a partnership is often accompanied by deep regret, even if you might not realize it amid your current lifestyle. Acknowledge that having your partner is far more critical than you may want to admit. Take your time.

Develop a strategy to break free from the double life and reclaim your partner's trust by utilizing the insights and tools provided in this book. The WTF (Enough) tool is here to help you take a stand and awaken from the potential losses you face if you continue on this destructive path. It's time to confront the reality and consequences of living a lie.

Understand that living a double life is rooted in deception, and deception is an irreparable lie. If you're concealing addictions such as drugs, alcohol, sex, or gambling, it's essential to recognize that these are deceptive lies and can have long-lasting, damaging effects. It's time to confront these issues head-on and seek the necessary help and support to break free from the cycle of deception and restore trust in your partnership.

Remember, by taking decisive action and committing to change, you can begin the process of healing and rebuilding a solid foundation of honesty and trust in your partnership.

202

The Ultimate Solution: You're Right, I'm Wrong Tool

In any situation where you desperately try to reclaim your partner, the ultimate solution beckons: "You're Right, I'm Wrong." This isn't just a casual phrase; it's a profound acknowledgment that you're willing to rectify the discord. Recognize the gravity of your partner's feelings, admit your mistakes without evasion, and commit to making amends. Despite the shared responsibility in a relationship, it's an admission that you're taking the initiative to mend the fractures.

If you've erred, don't shy away from accountability. Concealing or justifying your mistakes only deepens the wounds. Your path to redemption begins with the unreserved confession, "You're right, I'm wrong." It's a powerful declaration that signifies your readiness to rebuild and redefine your connection.

Mistakes are inevitable, but their impact intensifies when left unacknowledged or defended. Defensiveness breeds hostility and erodes trust. The "You're Right, I'm Wrong" mantra serves as the catalyst for healing, an admission that you're acknowledging your missteps and actively seeking to transform them into positive change.

Reflect on the decisions that led your relationship to its current state, own those decisions, and declare, "You're right; I'm wrong for not being on the same page. But it changes now." This isn't just a platitude; it's a call to action. Embrace this skill, grasp the power you hold to redirect the course of your relationship and decide to dwell in a partnership marked by joy.

Do you want to reside in a house where silence reigns and your partner's presence is a mere echo? Do you wish to spend your days in anger, brushing past each other like strangers? It's time to be the bigger person, utter the words: "You're right, I'm wrong," and apologize sincerely. Take these words beyond rhetoric – let them fuel your commitment to transformative change.

LOVE WINS when met with intentional, dedicated actions. It's not just about saying 'I love you'—it's about showing up, choosing your partner every day, and honoring the commitment even when it's hard. Love thrives when it's nurtured through presence, patience, and effort. Small, consistent gestures of kindness, understanding, and support build a bond that can weather life's storms. In the end, it's not grand declarations but the quiet, steady actions that prove love is real—and lasting

BONUS

Words you should never ever say to your partner

"Are you crazy?"
"Are you wearing that?"
"Calm down!"
"Don't be mad. I was just kidding!" "Don't take this the wrong way, but..."
"Get over it!"
"Give me space!"
"Hurry up!"
"I hate you!"
"I don't care."
"I told you..."
"If you don't like it, leave!"
"I'll do it later."
"I'm done."
"It's none of your business!"
"It's your fault!"
"You look tired."
"You need to go on a diet."
"You never let me do what I want." "You remind me of my mother."
"You should have asked for help." "You wouldn't understand."
"You're annoying."
"You're asking a lot of questions." "You're being ridiculous!"
"You're not listening to me."
"You're wrong."
"Relax."
"Shut up!"
"Stop crying!"
"Stop nagging me!"
"Stop talking!"
"That's not my job."
"What did you do all day?" "What's wrong now?"
"Why are you freaking out?"

Words you should
say more often to your partner

"I love you."

"I miss you."

"I need you."

"I'm sorry."

"I trust you."

"I love being with you."

"I love how you take care of me." "I love kissing you."

"I love our journey."

"I love the life we've created together."

"I love the way you carry yourself."

"I think you're simply beautiful."

"I'd do it all over again."

"I'll do the dishes."

"I'm crazy about you!"

"I'm happy with you."

"I'm so glad you're in my life."

"I'm so in love with you."

"I'm proud of you."

"I've got this."

"I've got you."

"You are everything to me."

"You bring out the best in me."

"You got this."

"You look great!"

"You make life easy."

"You make me want to be a better person."

"You're brilliant."

"You're great!"

"You're my best friend."

"You're so beautiful."

"You're the BEST!"

"You're the best thing that has ever happened to me." "You're right."

"What do you think?"

DEDICATION AND GRATITUDE

First, to the love of my life who has stood behind me as I went through my journey to complete this book and get it right.

To my guy friends: I want to thank you for your stories and experiences that I was able to share—Jim Ferris, John Pattyson, Leon Johnny Harris, Ron Burkhardt, Michael Todd.

To great family and friends that gave perspective on the book—thank you! Joannie Fair, Casey Fisher, Rayne Hagstrom, Aaron Iannello, Donna McCann PsyD, David Pfeiffer, Eileen Ney.

TESTIMONY

"You're Right, I'm Wrong is an eye-opening book that exposes human reactions to what triggers partnerships to drift. Most say awareness is half the battle. The author's use of wit and metaphors make this book relatable for couples to regain the fun, love, and re-build trust back into the partnership by bringing awareness to what created the issues. He shares his secrets and the tools to get the partnership back on track. This is a must-read."
Donna McCann, Psy.D., LMFT, Trauma Specialis

"I read this book during a rough patch in my marriage, and let me just say—it changed the game. It gave me a language for things I didn't even realize I was feeling. It's like sitting down with a wise, no-nonsense friend who also knows how to make you laugh when you need it most." — Elena Vargas, Reader and Small Business Owner

"A modern-day relationship manual that delivers clarity, compassion, and just the right amount of tough love. The metaphors are on point, the storytelling is vulnerable, and the advice is applicable whether you're newly in love or twenty years deep."— Tariq Bishop, Host of the "Mindful Men" Podcast

"This book helped me recognize where I was silently sabotaging my own relationship. 'You're Right, I'm Wrong' teaches accountability without shame and reminds us that humility isn't weakness—it's strength. Every couple should read this together." — Rachel Kim, Executive Coach and Relationship Facilitator

"This isn't just a book. It's a mirror, a wake-up call, and a toolbox all in one. Whether you're in a happy relationship or struggling to save one, there's something in here that will open your eyes."
— Danielle Rivera, Wellness Blogger and Longtime Reader

The QR code below
Will bring you to the Online Platform When you logon to
the Online Platform You will have access to the following:
Workbook with additional tools Lessons, Tips, and Examples
Motivational Couples Advice

www.youarerightiamwrong.com

It is all about making daily choices that are aligned with your
partner This book is all about helping you have
A great life and an amazing partnership

You can also buy the eBook format in Arabic, Chinese, English,
French, German, Hindi, Japanese, Korean, Portuguese, Russian,
Spanish

www.ingramcontent.com/pod-product-compliance
Lightning Source LLC
Chambersburg PA
CBHW060337100426
42812CB00003B/1033